BAPTISM
IN THE
Holy Spirit

GUILLERMO MALDONADO

Our Mission

Called to bring the supernatural power of God to this generation

Baptism in the Holy Spirit
2018 First Edition

ISBN 978-1-59272-715-5

All rights reserved by Ministerio Internacional El Rey Jesus

(King Jesus International Ministry).

This publication may not be reproduced, altered (in whole or part), archived in any electronic system nor transmitted by any electronic, mechanical (including photocopying or recording devices) or stored in any information storage retrieval system, or in any other manner, without the previous written permission by the author. Unless otherwise indicated, all Scripture quotations are taken from the New King James Version, © 1979, 1980, 1982, 1984 by Thomas Nelson, Inc. Used by permission.

Project Director: Andres Brizuela
Editors: Jose M. Anhuaman & Gloria Zura
Cover Design: Caroline Pereira
Interior Design: Jose M. Anhuaman

Published in Spanish with the title:
Bautismo en el Espíritu Santo

Translated to English by Henrry Becerra

King Jesus International Ministry
ERJ Publicaciones
14100 SW 144th Ave, Miami, FL 33186
Tel: (305) 382-3171 - Fax: (305) 675-5770

Printed in the United States of America

INDEX

Introduction	5
1. Who is the Holy Spirit?	7
2. The Purpose of Baptism in the Holy Spirit	42
3. The Outpouring of the Holy Spirit in the End Times	76
4. The Revelation of Gift of Tongues	116
About the Author	157

INTRODUCTION

The people of God are hungry and thirsty to know the Holy Spirit intimately. They feel the need to receive more from God and the passion to immerse themselves more in His presence. However, there are pastors and leaders around the world who do not give importance to this. They do not lead their congregations to be baptized by the Spirit or to receive His fullness.

Those who act this way tend to see the ministry as natural or a profession, so they seek shortcuts and use methods that do not require commitment, and which fail to change people's lives. They conform to the currents of public opinion and adapt to worldly methods, because they do not understand that ministry is supernatural and can only be developed with the support of God.

Why is it important to receive the Holy Spirit and be led by Him? Because He has always been present in every great event of mankind. Every time the Father is going to create or bring something new to the earth, He participates. Each time we want to see the power of God in action, He is the hand that carries it out. Every time the Father wants to show His glory, His Spirit is the one who opens the portals so that, like Ezekiel, we walk under "open heavens".

The Holy Spirit is the continuation of God on earth, who reveals Jesus Christ and His finished work on the cross. He is the promise of the Father and is the same power that acted in Jesus. Being baptized in the Holy Spirit is a sign of being separated and consecrated to serve the Lord. It is not the manifestation of a gift but of the very power of God.

Today I want to invite you to be baptized and receive the fullness of the Holy Spirit. This is a continual filling, until, as the Word says, rivers of living water flow from your spirit; until the dry areas of your life become springs of water that quench the thirst for everlasting life.

How will you know that you have been baptized in the Holy Spirit? In this book I explain it in detail, but I tell you now that you will leave behind your natural state and become a supernatural being. You will be empowered to do the things of God. Now, the key question is: Are you ready to be baptized in the Holy Spirit? If you are ready, start reading! Immerse yourself in His depths, and let the Spirit guide you.

1

Who is the Holy Spirit?

Throughout history, the enemy has subtly plotted and attempted to steal from the Church of Christ the supernatural character it was founded upon, and make it a natural entity. For this he has used various substitutes. That is, if the devil cannot make people stop believing in God and leave the church, he offers replacements to keep them entertained and deceived. Thus, people go to the temple, but they leave same or worse than they entered, because many churches have become dead entities, devoid of the life of the Spirit and of His power to overcome adversity.

In modern times, charisma and human talent have come to replace the baptism of the Holy Spirit. Many of today's leaders—in some cases out of ignorance and because they don't know better—use only their charisma, personality, or leadership to move their churches forward. They believe that they can do the work of God based on their personal talent. Unfortunately, they lack revelation of what ministry life means and the power it must manifest.

Many people believe in God, but not in baptism with the Holy Spirit. Even in certain Christian circles they feel that being baptized with Him is unnecessary, and replace His power with something that looks less shocking to others. Thus, they compromise and deny the truth to please people, even at the cost of displeasing the Lord. They try to supply their spiritual deficiencies in their own way and refuse to do so in the manner of God. If we want to live in, know and understand the truth, we need to begin by accepting it as it is and not as it suits us. The baptism with the Holy Spirit is a truth established by Christ and cannot be replaced or accommodated.

> *A church cannot say it walks in the truth of God, while still trying to please people instead of Him.*

In this first chapter I consider it a priority to establish who the Holy Spirit is; the place He occupies in the deity, and His role on the earth as well as in our lives. This way, if our desire is to live according, we will not fall or make mistakes out of ignorance.

- **The Holy Spirit is God Himself**

The Scripture establishes that there is one God, but He reveals Himself in three people, each one with a different function: The Father, the Son and the Holy Spirit. God the Father is the creator of all things. From Him come the heavens, the earth, and everything that dwells in them. No one has been able to see Him, but He reveals Himself to mankind through the person of His only begotten Son; Jesus is the Son of God. He is the revelation of the Father, who became a man and dwelled among us; and finally, the Holy Spirit is the administrator of the power of God and His revelation.

I do not understand how there are people who claim to believe in Jesus as their Lord and Savior, who read and respect the Word of God (the Bible), but deny the Holy Spirit and the need to be baptized by Him and receive His power. When the Holy Spirit is denied, Jesus is denied as well because they are one with the Father, and all three are the true God. Furthermore, the only person who can reveal Jesus is the Holy Spirit, as this is how Christ established it. When we deny or reject the Spirit and the things of Him (such as His fullness, baptism, and outpouring), we are denying the second coming of Christ and Jesus Himself.

- **The Holy Spirit is the continuation of God on the earth, in the now**

Another trait that the Holy Spirit shares with the Father and the Son is that He is eternal. The three are one and the same God; It means that they are, live and operate in the eternal present. The Spirit of God does not live in the past, nor was He assigned only to ancient times; He is the current and present reality. He is the truth and wants to reveal Himself to us now, in the 21st century; not as an agent of the past, but as a divine ambassador for today.

> *If we teach truths in past times, there is no power to produce what we preach. The Holy Spirit is not history; He is the power of God in the present.*

■ The Holy Spirit reveals Jesus Christ to us and His finished work on the cross

In the Old Testament, we see the Father in action, manifesting Himself to the people of Israel, demonstrating His power, giving direction and using the voice of the prophets to prepare the way for His Son. Then arose Jesus Christ, the Redeemer, the Messiah announced in Scripture; with a specific assignment to manifest the Lord to us. However, He had to pay the full price to restore mankind to a genuine and direct relationship with the Father, like what Adam and Eve had before they sinned and fell short of the glory of God. Then came the Holy Spirit, to bring that reality to the heart of every person who accepts Christ and His finished work on the cross. *"When the Day of Pentecost had fully come, they were all with one accord in one place. And suddenly there came a sound from heaven, as of a rushing mighty wind, and it filled the whole house where they were sitting"* (Acts 2:1-2).

■ The Holy Spirit is the promise of the Father

In the Old Testament, the Father promised to send us the person of the Holy Spirit when He spoke, *"And it shall come to pass afterward that I will pour out My Spirit on all flesh..."* (Joel 2:28). In the New Testament, apostle Paul refers to this verse in Galatians 3:14, affirming that Jesus made Himself a curse for us to receive His blessing, *"That we might receive the promise of the Spirit through faith."* The Father confirmed this as part of His promise in the restoration of Israel, when He spoke through prophet Ezekiel and said: *"I will give you a new heart and put a new spirit within you; I will take the heart of stone out of your flesh and give you a heart of flesh. I will put My Spirit within you and cause you to walk in My statutes, and you will keep My judgments and do them"* (Ezekiel 36:26-27).

Also in the New Testament, Jesus Christ made a reference to this promise from the Father and told His disciples: *"...I send the Promise of My Father upon you..."* (Luke 24:49). The Son came to earth to place His Spirit upon mankind once more, as it was in the beginning when, *"The Lord God formed man of the dust of the ground, and breathed into his nostrils the breath of life; and man became a living being"* (Genesis 2:7). Jesus brought the Father's promises to pass. He gave us the Holy Spirit, so that He may dwell in us and take us ack to the life that Adam lost in Eden.

■ The Holy Spirit is the power that worked in Jesus

After His resurrection, Jesus met with His disciples and said to them: *"And now I will send the Holy Spirit, just as my Father promised. But stay here in the city until the Holy Spirit comes and fills you with power from heaven"* (Luke 24:49 - NLT). Jesus was specific with regards to the aspect of the Holy Spirit they were to receive; He told them that they would receive power. Hence the emphasis of all activity and movement of the early church was the manifestation of the supernatural power of God, and the source of that power is the Holy Spirit. He is that power!

In fact, Jesus ordered His disciples to remain in Jerusalem until they received the Spirit of God. He did not give them options, but an order, because it was necessary that they be clothed in power. Jesus knew that the miraculous power of God was a requirement for His disciples to be His legal witnesses.

In the previous verse, to be *"endued"* means to be *"clothed with or in"*. It refers to the mantle of the Holy Spirit. This happens when one is baptized with the Spirit of the living

God. At this moment, the believer receives the mantle of the Holy Spirit, covering him with power from heaven and transforming him into a carrier of it. When speaking of power, the Scripture refers to miracle-working power. In other words, Jesus told His disciples, "You do not leave here until you are clothed in the miracle-working mantle that will allow you to continue My work here on earth."

WHAT IS BAPTISM WITH THE HOLY SPIRIT AND POWER?

"Then I remembered the word of the Lord, how He said: John indeed baptized with water, but you shall be baptized with the Holy Spirit" (ACTS 11:16).

In Greek, to be "baptized" is translated as baptizo. This word was used, for example, when water was drawn from a well and a kind of bucket was tied at the end of a rope, then the rope was given slack until the container was completely submerged in the water of the well. The act of submerging the bucket completely in the well water was known as baptism. People then said that the bucket had been baptized. The term was also used to refer to what happened when, in the middle of a storm on the high seas, a ship was completely covered by a great wave. The full immersion of the boat in the water was also known as "baptism". Thus, when the time came for people to be fully submerged in water, as a sign of having recognized Jesus as their Lord and Savior, it was also called "baptism."

In the same way, the baptism with the Holy Spirit is to be totally submerged or immersed in the supernatural power of God; This is something that happens once in a lifetime. On the contrary, the fullness of the Holy Spirit is an experience that must be lived continuously. This is because, as we serve God and His people, we will have battles that can only be won through His power.

In the case of the coming of the Holy Spirit on a person, the same word is used to imply what lies within him, that gift of God that comes upon the individual, filling their spirit until it overflows and covering them completely. The baptism of the Holy Spirit means that we are totally covered by Him, completely submerged in the waters of the Spirit. It is important to note that here, you are not possessing the Holy Spirit, but the Holy Spirit is possessing you, without measure. He is the one who contains you, while you have Him in the measure that you continue to be filled.

The baptism with the Holy Spirit is a supernatural atmosphere that spills over a man or woman who has identified with Christ in His death and resurrection. Whenever a believer who has been baptized with the Holy Spirit goes anywhere, that baptism is evident in the supernatural atmosphere he carries and manifests. Whenever he sees a need or an impossibility, he manifests the supernatural, because the heart of God is activated before the need of the human being, and wants to make himself known by supplying it.

This supernatural activity can heal the sick, cast out demons, and give words of knowledge and prophecy; it has the power to set people free from demonic oppression, heal the wounded heart and break the chains of bitterness and hatred. It can soften a heart hardened by pain, supply a financial need and make possible what seems impossible to man. In short, the believer can manifest the power of God in the area where the person who does not know him is most in need.

Throughout my time in ministry, I have met several leaders who were filled and baptized with the Holy Spirit. Many began their ministry with an outpouring of His power, but as time passed, they ceased to be filled and the outpouring stopped. This did not happen overnight, but progressively, as they made modifications in their church to fit the opinion of the people, seeking to please others, and not be criticized or rejected. Without realizing it, they lost the fire; they traded it for charisma and talent, because these are more accepted by people who seek a spiritual experience adjusted to their own requirements.

How do I know this? Because the things that happened at the beginning of their ministry, no longer happen; the power of the Spirit they manifested at first is now absent, and the only atmosphere that can be breathed is one of religiosity and stagnation. Their churches no longer want the Holy Spirit, nor do they want any supernatural manifestation that His presence can bring. Their lives are stagnant and they are short of the power and fullness of the Spirit of God. If this applies to you, and what you read is convicting you, I encourage you to return to the source; I invite you to refill yourself with the Holy Spirit and let Him participate in His ministry as the steward of revelation and the power of God.

> *The baptism with the Holy Spirit is a sign of having been separated and consecrated to serve God.*

As we defined above, baptism is an authorization from God to demonstrate His power, to reveal and show the work of His Son. On the cross, Jesus Christ was wounded for our transgressions and rebellions (Isaiah 53: 3-6). There, He crucified sin, sickness, demonic oppression, poverty and everything that bound us. Jesus paid the price of our rebellion and gave us His forgiveness, holiness, healing and inheritance as children of God. Therefore, now that we are filled with the Holy Spirit, we are also called to possess the authority that Jesus delegated to us.

We can do what Jesus did, demonstrating the power of God and making effective the defeat of Satan. We can heal the sick, free the captives, raise the dead, break the slavery of poverty, and release supernatural provision; So that all may see the living and almighty God who acts in us and through us. We can do all this because we have received the authorization and legal right to use the power of God and demonstrate all that Christ gained on the cross.

WHAT IS SUPERNATURAL POWER?

In the book of the Acts of the Apostles, we continually see how the people who received Christ were baptized with the Holy Spirit and His power. The apostles taught that same baptism because they knew its importance. Before that, even the disciples who had walked with Jesus in the flesh still failed to fully understood who He was. It was the Holy Spirit who revealed to the Son of God.

Before the power of the Holy Spirit came upon them, the disciples were a group of shy people, mostly fishermen, and completely unprepared to carry out their assignment on earth. For example, Peter, prior to being baptized with the Holy Spirit, denied Christ thrice for fear of losing his life, but when the Holy Spirit came upon him, he was filled with audacity, to the point that he stood before a multitude to preach the gospel of the Kingdom, and after his first preaching, three thousand people were added to them (Acts 2:41).

Before continuing, the first thing we must establish is that God is a supernatural being with supernatural abilities. He cannot be defined otherwise. That means He is above and beyond the natural limits, and it leads us to conclude that, if God is supernatural, His power is also supernatural.

The supernatural imparted by the Holy Spirit is the miraculous power of God, which is above and beyond all natural power. It operates above the laws of nature; that is, it is not governed by them, but transcends them and is located above and beyond time, space and matter. It is a power that does not belong to this world, and requires human beings to be washed by the blood of Christ, to gain legal access on earth. The supernatural power of God is also spiritual, invisible, eternal and unlimited; His is a power that surpasses the test of time.

> *Without the supernatural power of God we cannot supply the needs of people on this earth.*

God's plan is for the church to live and walk in His supernatural power. However, many times, the church is its own enemy, reducing its members to the natural dimension. Remember that God is supernatural; He intervenes in our world, but He is not of this world. It is time to remove the limits that we imposed on ourselves and let God be God. There is a reason why one of His names is the Almighty, and it is because He is greater than any circumstance and capable of overcoming the impossibilities presented to us in the natural dimension.

The supernatural power of God is creative and can work any miracle. We define it this way because it exceeds what we can do in our natural capacity as human beings. This is the power that created everything out of nothing. The power of God manifested brought about the heavens, the earth, the oceans, mountain, stars, our moon and our sun. John the apostle confirmed this in the vision mentioned in Revelation, when he said: *"You are worthy, O Lord, to receive glory and honor and power; for You created all things, and by Your will they exist and were created"* (Revelation 4:11). As we can see, God is the origin and creator of all things.

Many people have no trouble believing that God created the world, but they find it hard to believe that He can create something in the present. Today, I want you to receive the revelation that the same power that acted in the beginning—when the world and humanity were created—is available to continue creating. It can create an eye for whoever needs it, flesh in the body of one who has lost it, and bones, kidneys, teeth, legs, and so on. The Lord can also heal an organ that doctors have declared incurable, or make a document appear that does not exist and is needed; not by magic, but because He has power and dominion over everything created.

This is the case of Jeffrey and his wife, who are faithful members of our congregation in Miami. They spent six years praying and believing for their legal documents to reside in the United States. They never stopped giving their tithes and firstfruits to God. When they had their appointment before immigration, the officer who attended them told them that they were missing a document, therefore they would not receive the documents of legal residence. He also informed them that they would be deported. When their lawyer reviewed the case, he did not know what to do because that document did not exist. They were not discouraged and instead began to pray. Jeffrey and his wife asked the Holy Spirit of God to intervene. Then, the lawyer entered the official immigration website to review the case, and to his surprise, their residency was approved! That means that the important missing document supernaturally appeared, allowing the case to be approved. But it was not just that. Six years of sowing, faith and prayer continued to bear fruit. The owner of the company where Jeffrey worked decided to sell it and the new owners wanted to fire all the staff. Then came another buyer who finally acquired the company, and he asked Jeffrey to stay and offered to partner with him. Now, Jeffrey believes God will transfer the entire business to his hands.

"...*Twice I have heard this: That power belongs to God*" (Psalms 62:11). The power of God originates in Him and there are no limits to what He is capable of. However, man prefers to seek his own way. The fallen nature of man deceives him to act independently of God, seeking other ways to solve his problems and in his own ability. However, the power of God is available to everyone who believes.

> **There is no supernatural fullness that lasts forever.**

THE MANIFESTATION OF THE HOLY SPIRIT IS NOT THE MANIFESTATION OF A GIFT, BUT OF THE POWER OF GOD

Nowadays, when speaking of the baptism with the Holy Spirit, traditional theology places more emphasis on speaking in new tongues than on the power of God this baptism releases. Religion values His gifts, but leaves aside the power, which is one of the most outstanding characteristics of God and can do what no one else on earth is capable of. That power is transferred to us through baptism with the Holy Spirit.

In reviewing Scripture, we see that tongues are just an initial evidence. Tongues are given to pray beyond reason, to build up our spirit and our faith. But the emphasis should not be on the gift of tongues but on the power of God. I know many who speak tongues and lack power. They do not cast out demons, they do not heal the sick and many even live in depression. There are those who prophesy, but their words are not backed by manifestations of the power of God. They speak of the future, because they have no power to manifest God in the now.

When someone is baptized with the Holy Spirit, he receives the power of God and His love consumes that person. That is why we see that the pattern of the book of Acts is repeated, where the church grew as many were saved, then baptized in water, then filled and baptized with the Holy Spirit and taught the Word of God.

If the Word is placed above the Spirit, the pattern is wrong. The Spirit moved first and God spoke later (Genesis 1:1). That is the pattern we must bring to new believers, to receive Jesus into their hearts, to be filled with the Holy Spirit and then to learn the Word. That is how they will remain in the church, because the revelation that the Holy Spirit gives them of the Word will bring real changes in their inner being. If they do not receive the Spirit, every process these new believers go through will be mental and not spiritual. Only when they are filled with the Holy Spirit are they born again into the spirit world. *"...unless one is born of water and the Spirit, he cannot enter the kingdom of God. That which is born of* the flesh is flesh, and that which is born of the Spirit is spirit" (John 3:5-6).

EVIDENCE OF BAPTISM WITH THE HOLY SPIRIT AND POWER

Just as there are signs of being born again, there is also evidence that someone has been baptized with the Holy Spirit. I have mentioned some already, but I will dedicate this section to developing the point in more detail. These are some of the signs of being baptized in the Holy Spirit and His power:

1. The believer goes through a super naturalized state.

When the Spirit comes upon a believer, he is supernaturalized because that is the nature of the Spirit of God. He is supernatural and everything that comes in contact with him becomes supernatural. This is proof that the power of God is there produce supernatural works (miracles, signs and wonders) whenever and wherever he goes. Every believer baptized with the Holy Spirit lives in a supernatural state and things happen to him like what Peter and John experienced in the book of Acts.

Now Peter and John went up together to the temple at the hour of prayer, the ninth hour. And a certain man lame from his mother's womb was carried, whom they laid daily at the gate of the temple which is called Beautiful, to ask alms from those who entered the temple; who, seeing Peter and John about to go into the temple, asked for alms. And fixing his eyes on him, with John, Peter said, 'Look at us.' So he gave them his attention, expecting to receive something from them. Then Peter said, 'Silver and gold I do not have, but what I do have I give you: In the name of Jesus Christ of Nazareth, rise up and walk.' And he took him by the right hand and lifted him up, and immediately his feet and ankle bones received strength. (ACTS 3:1-7)

Apostle Paul was a man who lived full of the Holy Spirit. He would heal the sick and impart the Spirit of God over new believers. *"And when Paul had laid hands on them, the Holy Spirit came upon them, and they spoke with tongues and prophesied... Now God worked unusual miracles by the hands of Paul"* (Acts 19:6, 11). Here we see that Paul was supernaturalized. Upon arriving to Ephesus, he laid hands upon the believers and all were filled with the Holy Spirit. After that, he dedicated himself to preaching the gospel without ceasing, and the Word says that God worked extraordinary miracles through him.

> **When we live in a supernaturalized state, we operate in the power of God at will.**

When we are filled with the Holy Spirit, we live in a state of supernatural energy. You may be physically exhausted, but once the supernatural power of God begins to flow, you are filled with an energy greater than yourself. That force does not come from our physical body or the food we eat, but from Holy Spirit.

> *One of the signs we have been filled with the Holy Spirit is living in a supernatural-ized state, saturated and energized with the power of God.*

2. The person is consumed with passion for God.

Other unequivocal evidence that a person has been baptized with the Holy Spirit is that their passion for God increases; for seeking His presence, His Word, holiness, for prayer, His power, and for manifesting this to others. All that person wants is to have God, His power and His presence. When someone is baptized by the Holy Spirit he develops a greater passion for God, to receive more of the Lord and become one with Him in passion and purpose. The believer begins to love what God loves and hate what He hates, because he shares one Spirit with Him. That person is willing to live and die for Christ; he wants to announce it to the world, even if in doing so he must suffer. The person that has been baptized in the

Holy Spirit desires to demonstrate His power and love to all, as he goes through daily life. His passion is such that the things of God becomes his priority.

The passion Jus had for the Father and for mankind is what led him to the cross. He was indifferent to none of us, *"But when He saw the multitudes, He was moved with compassion for them, because they were weary and scattered, like sheep having no shepherd"* (Matthew 9:36). His life was filled with passion for everyone to find salvation, know the Father and be reconciled into the family of God. The baptism with the Holy Spirit has the virtue of infecting us with that same passion.

> **Passion for God releases His fire over your life.**

This happened to Kevin, who traveled from Palm Beach, Florida, United States, to one of my meetings. He testifies: "Some time ago, doctors diagnosed me with grade III chronic kidney disease, because my kidneys only worked at 40% of their capacity. I was told I would need dialysis and eventually a transplant. One day my wife and I learned that the Apostle Maldonado would be in West Palm Beach for a conference, and we believed that God could heal me. Something wonderful happened there. As the musicians sang, I got lost in worship. I began to praise God and push to get deeper into His presence, until everything around me disappeared. It was as if I was alone with the Lord, everything else went out of my mind and I simply worshiped Him. Convinced that God would do something, I said to my wife, 'Today I leave this place healed!' Then the apostle said that if anyone had kidney problems to stand up, come in agreement with him and believe for a miracle. He prayed and I felt a strong heat in my back around my kidneys. My wife touched my back and could feel the heat in her hands. It was not my imagination, it was real! I left the place convinced that God had healed me. However, a few weeks later, I had a diabetic coma. I arrived at the hospital having lost my vision, the ability to speak and I could hardly walk, and had to be admitted in the intensive care unit.

The doctors told my wife that with such an advanced stage of kidney disease that, I should have suffered from brain damage or be dead. But when they saw my scans, they were amazed and said, 'This is incredible! Your medical history shows you have a grade III kidney disease, but on ultrasound your kidneys are perfect! They look like those of an 18-year-old, and they're running at 100 percent efficiency.' That's why I did not die, because my kidneys were pumping sugar out of my system. The doctors said it could only be a miracle. That night, in West Palm Beach, the Holy Spirit filled me with passion for God, and I was completely healed! Today, I continue walking passionate for the Lord. At home, we decided to turn off the television and make our home an altar of worship. Since then, our families and neighbors are reaching the feet of Christ."

3. Jesus becomes a complete reality in your life.

When the Holy Spirit baptizes a person, He takes full control and becomes more real to them than anything else. This is another clear evidence that baptism has taken place. Before, the person was more aware of his problems, of himself, of what he wanted to have, of what he lacked; of offenses, compliments, criticism and recognitions. He was more aware of the opinion of others, of the world, of what it could offer him; of money, of possessions, of temporary success, and so on. But when the Holy Spirit baptizes someone, all of shifts to second place, and the person becomes more aware of God. Then, the Holy Spirit will be for that person more real than the disease, more real than the offenses, than the earthly success and everything else.

Paul taught the Colossians this when he wrote: *"Set your mind on things above, not on things on the earth"* (Colossians 3:2). This is only possible when the Holy Spirit comes upon a person, because our reality shifts to the "things above", and not the ones on earth.

4. The believer becomes consumed by the love of God.

When the Holy Spirit baptizes a believer, He makes a radical change in his heart; removing the selfishness and pride of the "old man" and bringing the heart of God, which is full of genuine love. In his letter to the Romans, Paul affirms that: *"Hope does not disappoint, because the love of God has been poured out in our hearts by the Holy Spirit who was given to us"* (Romans 5:5). I believe that there is no other real way to the supernatural than the love of God. The fundamental motive of the Father in giving us His Spirit and His power is love.

> *Love is the path to supernatural power.*

Everything God does is driven by love. That is His engine. This love leads us to demonstrate His power wherever we go. Without love, we do not care about our neighbor's need, their pain does not move us and we have no mercy of their suffering. Without the love of God we cannot use His power, because our motivations would be selfish. Selfishness corrupts the power God gives us to meet the needs of others and witness to Jesus.

> **One of the clearest signs that the baptism with the Holy Spirit has taken place in the heart of a believer is his or her love for God.**

Pastor Alejandro of Uruguay testifies to this: "Our country was known as a graveyard for preachers because no ministry lasted long there. Most congregations did not exceed forty people. It was an apathetic, traditional country and its strongest mark was unbelief. My family has a church and a school in a modest area of Montevideo, the capital. For twenty years, we worked in the ministry, without having a spiritual covering (a spiritual father who would impart to us, empower us and send us in the ministry), and after all that time we only reached a hundred members. We were exhausted, thinking that everything was lost. We could not take the burden anymore and we were about to give up. However, when my wife and I arrived at King Jesus we were amazed by the ministry of Apostle Maldonado, and began to feel hungry to move in the supernatural and to have the heart of God. Then the Holy Spirit began to impart His love and strength over us. We understood the power of spiritual fatherhood. Our daughters were set free from rebellion and are now on fire for God. In fact, the supernatural manifests itself in the church the most among the youth. The revelation of God's paternity and spiritual fatherhood led us to break the curse that kept churches from growing in our territory. That new love made people begin to take root in the church. Before, they came and went, but now spiritual children began to develop with revelation of God's fatherhood.

Then came a spiritual revival and miracles began to happen in all areas. One of the most shocking happened to one of our spiritual daughters, who gave birth to her baby practically dead. His lungs and heart did not work and the doctors gave her no hope. But my wife and I came together in the waiting room and prayed, decreeing healing for the newborn in the name of Jesus. A few days later the baby left the intensive care in perfect condition. The power of God healed him! His father and the rest of the family did not believe in miracles, but after seeing what God did, they surrendered their lives to Christ. We are so grateful for that impartation of the Spirit of love and power that transformed us forever. Today the love of God consumes us! It has filled our heart, renewed our strength, increased our faith and makes us want to continue. Our congregation has multiplied and the same has happened in finances, in evangelism, in miracles, in everything! We want more of God, of His Spirit; more miracles, signs and growth!"

> *The evidence that a believer has been baptized with the Holy Spirit is His power; speaking in tongues is only the first sign.*

THE DIFFERENCE BETWEEN BEING BORN OF THE SPIRIT AND BAPTIZED WITH THE SPIRIT

Most believers do not know the difference between being born of the Spirit and being baptized with Him. Some believe it is the same experience. Others think that being born again is more than enough and that baptism with the Holy Spirit was only for the direct disciples of Jesus, so that they would start the church. Others have not even thought of this and see Christianity as one more religion, a belief, a doctrine, and a set of rules to be fulfilled to win God's favor, but are disconnected from Him. However, it is important to know the difference in the light of Scripture, and if you are missing either one of these experiences, you can live them today.

Jesus said to Nicodemus, Pharisee and judge among the Jews: *"Most assuredly, I say to you, unless one is born again, he cannot see the kingdom of God."* (John 3:3). The term "born again" refers to the fact that, because of sin, man suffered an irreversible spiritual death. The only way to return to life is to receive it again through the Spirit of God and the sacrifice of Jesus Christ on the cross. His death symbolized ours and His resurrection is the force or power that resurrects us or leads us to "be born again." This means that the fall of man was erased, his sin was forgiven and all debt was paid on the cross.

Being "Born again" means that we are justified and transferred to the state of innocence that Adam had at the beginning, as if we had never sinned. The sacrifice of Christ brings us back to the original state. The new birth reconnects our spirit with the Spirit of God, by taking the breath of life He gives us through His Holy Spirit.

After being risen, one of the first actions Jesus took was to give His disciples the Spirit of life, the one who came to resurrect their dead spirits. *"So Jesus said to them again, 'Peace to you! As the Father has sent Me, I also send you.' And when He had said this, He breathed on them, and said to them: Receive the Holy Spirit"* (John 20:21-22). This was what led them to be born again, meaning they now had the same life God gave to Adam at the time of creation, when the Father blew His divine breath over a body made from the dust of the earth.

From that moment on, their sins were forgiven, they had free access to the Father and the life of the Spirit. Therefore, they would go to heaven and their name would be written in the book of life. After this new birth, Christ asked them to wait in Jerusalem, for the Father would send them to the Holy Spirit so that they would be empowered to become His witnesses.

In other words, the new birth is receiving the life of the Spirit, but it does not qualify the believer to be a witness or authorize him to use the power of God; Otherwise they should not have waited until the day of Pentecost.

Jesus knew that for His disciples to be witnesses they had to receive the baptism with the Holy Spirit. Many have received the first breath, which is to be born again, with the right to be called "children of God", but they have not lived the second experience.

> *The first impartation of the Holy Spirit is the life of God, as it was in the beginning. The second breath—which is the baptism—is where He gives us His power.*

The same thing happened with Jesus. Even though He was born without sin He still had to be baptized and empowered by the Holy Spirit before carrying out His sacrifice on the cross. The baptism of Jesus with the Holy Spirit occurred the same day He was baptized in the waters of the Jordan by John the Baptist. *"When all the people were baptized, it came to pass that Jesus also was baptized; and while He prayed, the heaven was opened. And the Holy Spirit descended in bodily form like a dove upon Him, and a voice came from heaven which said, 'You are My beloved Son; in You I am well pleased.' Now Jesus Himself began His ministry at about thirty years of age, being (as was supposed) the son of Joseph, the son of Heli"* (Luke 3:21-23).

Jesus was born of the Spirit, having been conceived by the Spirit of God in the womb of Mary (Luke 1:35).

However, He did not demonstrate the power of God with miracles, signs and wonders until he was baptized with the Holy Spirit in the Jordan when He was about thirty years old. We know that Christ was not under the nature of sin, because He was not begotten by Joseph but by the Spirit of God. Unlike Him, we have a sinful nature because we were born of a natural mother and father and were conceived with an inheritance of sin that has been transferred from generation to generation. Therefore, we all need to be "born again" from the Spirit, because only then can we be originated from God. That is the mystery of the new birth, and Nicodemus could not understand because it was not revealed to him.

In many Bible schools and institutes this point is argued and many believe that "being born again" is the same as being baptized with the Holy Spirit. Yes, the one who intervenes is the same Spirit, but His operation is different. So, is it the same thing to be born again than to be baptized with the Spirit? Of course not! The Scripture is very clear in that the baptism in waters and the baptism with the Holy Spirit was what marked the beginning of the ministry of Jesus, several years after He was born of the Spirit.

I know many churches and ministries that are content to simply be "born again" and be saved, thinking they don't need anything more. I do not say that the new birth is not the most wonderful miracle that Jesus could have done for us. He gave us new life to reconcile us to the

Father, but He also gave us a commission to be fulfilled here on earth. That task can only be done with the power imparted by the Holy Spirit when He baptizes us, when He comes upon us and covers us completely. Churches that walk only with the new birth are doing nothing for God, or at least they are not doing it in the way, in the strengths or in the power of God, as Jesus did. The reason is that these believers are not baptized with the Spirit, who empowers us to do the work of Jesus Christ here on earth.

> *When you are baptized with Holy Spirit you become a credible witness because you can prove your testimony.*

When you are born of the Spirit you still do not have the ability to prove that God is real and alive, or to be a witness of Jesus Christ. A good example is that of Moses, because until the Angel of the Lord appeared to him in the burning bush, he could not preach to Israel and Pharaoh the will of God to deliver His people, or of His power to do it (Exodus 3: 2, Acts 7:35).

I believe that now you can better understand why the church is as it is, why so many Christians who love God are not effective witnesses of Jesus; why so many believers who love and serve Christ are still bound by sin. They can do not know how to overcome poverty, disease or the works of the flesh. We have many people born of the Spirit, sons and daughters of God, who are saved and going to heaven, but who are still not activated in the power to transform lives and perform miracles because they have not been baptized with the Holy Spirit. That is why they are not moving in the supernatural power, casting out demons, healing the sick and freeing the captives.

DIFFERENCE BETWEEN BEING FULL OF THE SPIRIT AND BEING BAPTIZED WITH HIM.

In the early church, the first to receive this promise were the disciples of Jesus. They were gathered in one accord when, *"They were all filled with the Holy Spirit and began to speak with other tongues, as the Spirit gave them utterance."* (Acts 2:4). This first fullness was so important that the apostles were always making sure the new Christians received it, both Jews and Gentiles; that is, both the children of the promise and those who did not belong to the chosen people of God. For example, on one occasion the apostle Paul came to the city of Ephesus and saw there about twelve men who had believed in Jesus but had not yet received the Holy Spirit, *"He said to them, 'Did you receive the Holy Spirit when you believed?' So they said to him, 'We have not so much as heard whether there is a*

Holy Spirit.' [...] And when Paul had laid hands on them, the Holy Spirit came upon them, and they spoke with tongues and prophesied" (Acts 19:2, 6).

The term "being full" indicates that there is a measure or a certain capacity cap. That measure is given by the space each one has in his life for the Holy Spirit to occupy. In the fullness He enters us, while in baptism, we are submerged in Him, and there is no limit. Many people in the modern church are operating in the fullness of the Spirit, but they have not been baptized. Then they operate within the limits they have set for the Spirit in them, but they still have control. They have not yielded complete and absolute control to Him.

I want you to know this difference, because as you read these pages, you can be baptized and filled with the Holy Spirit, to move into a supernatural state and be empowered to manifest God on earth through His miraculous power. Have you been saved? Have you been filled with the Holy Spirit? Have you been baptized in Him? Are you operating on earth with His supernatural power, with visible manifestations like miracles, signs and wonders? Today, right now, you can receive all that!

Jesus' disciples received the fullness of the Holy Spirit when He rose again and appeared before them. Then, *"He breathed on them, and said to them: Receive the Holy Spirit"* (John 20:22). We know that this was not baptism with the Holy Spirit, because He Himself told them to wait for the promise of the Father, whose fulfillment we see happening in Acts, after Jesus had risen to heaven. This means that when He breathed on them they were not baptized, but were born again and were filled with the Spirit of God. The experience where we are filled with the Holy Spirit is related to salvation, because it gives us eternal life, revives our spirit that was dead and allows the Spirit of God to dwell within us. He also gives us conviction of sin, and the strength and desire to walk in holiness. This is where the Holy Spirit fulfills His function as Counselor and Comforter, revealing the Father and Jesus Christ to us.

For you to understand more clearly, I present you with a list of the difference between the fullness and the baptism with the Holy Spirit:

- The fullness depends on the space or capacity the person yields for the Holy Spirit to occupy. But in baptism there is no limit because it is He who contains the person.

- In the fullness, the person is the one that controls everything, while in baptism the person lets go so that the Holy Spirit can grab a hold of everything.

- In the fullness, the Christian carries the Holy Spirit. In the baptism, el Holy Spirit possesses the person completely.

- When something is full but not overflowing, it is because what lies inside is not flowing, springing forth or rushing out.

There is an order in which we receive the different manifestations of the Holy Spirit in our life, and it is the following:

1. *The new birth:* This is the breath of the Spirit to receive eternal life and be reconciled with the Father through His Son. This is where we are filled for the first time.

2. *The fullness of the Holy Spirit:* This is to be filled with the Spirit of God every time we seek Him. It can be repeated unlimited times throughout our life. In the measure that we empty or pour ourselves out over others, He fills us again.

3. *The baptism with the Holy Spirit:* This is a unique event where we are submerged fully in Him, and where He imparts to us the power of God.

4. *The outpouring of the Holy Spirit:* It is the even that brings the fullness of the Spirit over all men and women of a region or continent. It is a mighty rush of the Spirit.

5. *The overflow:* This happens after the Spirit pours Himself out, until He overflows and impacts the world (Psalms 23:5). Here, the Holy Spirit has complete control.

From all the above we can conclude that, one can be full and not have been baptized with the Holy Spirit. In fact, many Christians around the world are full, but they have never been baptized. And among those who are full, many do not know what to do with that fullness. They do not know how to pour themselves or empty themselves into others to manifest the supernatural of God and to fill themselves again in His presence. In addition, a believer may be full and manifest the power of God, but still have not yielded total control of his life to the Spirit of God.

I close this chapter by asking you, do you want fullness or baptism with the Holy Spirit? Do you want the Holy Spirit in you to be limited or unlimited? Do you want Him to own you or do you prefer to keep control of your life in your hands? Your answers to these questions will determine what the Spirit does in you from now on.

2

The Purpose of Baptism in the Holy Spirit

The Church of Christ was born in the midst of the greatest revival ever produced by the Holy Spirit, and met the needs and impossibilities of the people. As a demonstration of the limitless power of God, there were miracles, signs and wonders. According to the book of Acts, the early Church provoked frequent commotion, and God always surprised them. Paul and the disciples of Jesus lived those experiences; that is why the Church grew and expanded strongly around the world, marking a before and after in the history of mankind.

However, the mentality of today's world has infiltrated the modern Church and reached the point where, instead of casting out demons, we tolerate them and even give them "counseling." We turn a blind eye and let people continue living in sin, feeding their old nature. As a result, we preach a watered-down gospel, where a half-truth is spoken so as not to offend others; where the work of Jesus on the cross is no longer the center of the Christian life, and where there is no power of the Holy Spirit to change the hearts of people. In fact, preachers and believers are even asked to respect the sinful nature of others, instead of seeking the will and holiness of God.

What was Jesus' original intention in giving the Church the baptism with the Holy Spirit? Surely it was not only for us to dance, exalt Him, raise our hands or clap in His name. These are all positive actions, but they are not the main purpose of the baptism with the Holy Spirit. In the light of the Scriptures, I have concluded that there were five essential reasons in God's plan:

1. Authorizes us to exercise power and authority

Jesus cast out demons with the power and authority that the Holy Spirit gave Him. He healed the sick because He was authorized by the Father: *"But if I cast out demons with the finger of God, surely the kingdom of God has come upon you"* (Luke 11:20). God gave Him the legal right to do so. But that did not end with His mission on earth, since Jesus transferred that same right to His disciples: *"Behold, I give you the authority to trample on serpents and scorpions, and over all the power of the enemy, and nothing shall by any means hurt you"* (Luke 10:19).

As believers, you and I are authorized to heal the sick, cast out demons, perform miracles, and take dominion over all created things, according to the will of God. We have power to put Satan and his demons under the soles of our feet, as well as authority to destroy all his works. We are vessels of honor that carry the authority of God, and are bearers of His supernatural power wherever we go. It is written: *"But as many as received Him, to them He gave the right to become children of God, to those who believe in His name"* (John 1:12).

> **When we don't demonstrate what we preach, the devil accuses us because he knows we are illegal witnesses.**

The great commission Jesus gave His disciples was: As you go, preach, saying, *'The kingdom of heaven is at hand.' Heal the sick, cleanse the lepers, raise the dead, cast out demons. Freely you have received, freely give"* (Matthew 10:7-8). Jesus never announced the gospel without casting out demons; and as soon as these saw Him, they began to become restless and violent. Neither did He preach the Kingdom without miracles. People sought Jesus because they felt that power was coming from Him, that He acted with authority and lived in holiness (1 John 3:8).

> *The baptism in the Holy Spirit is the backing and support we receive from God to fight against the enemy.*

2. Authorize us to demonstrate the finished work of the cross.

Apostle Paul saw that human words could not compete in strength or power to that which comes from God, and that there is nothing more powerful than to preach the finished work of Jesus on the cross. However, we need the Spirit to reveal our message to the hearts of the people. That is why in his first letter to the Corinthians, he told them: *"And my speech and my preaching were not with persuasive words of human wisdom, but in demonstration of the Spirit and of power, that your faith should not be in the wisdom of men but in the power of God"* (1 Corinthians 2:4-5).

What did Christ gain on the cross? Among many other benefits, Jesus conquered salvation, healing, deliverance, prosperity and transformation for the entire human race. However, He left us the task of demonstrating those works with the power of His Holy Spirit.

Jesus carried all our diseases to the cross so that we may be healed. Therefore, where there is disease, you have authority to bring healing. He bore all our oppressions so that we might be delivered; meaning that wherever there is spiritual, emotional or mental oppression, you have authority to bring freedom. He took all our faults, sins and shame so that we may be forgiven and receive His holiness; therefore, where someone is bound by sin and apart from God, you have authority to bring salvation. Jesus became poor so that we might be enriched; and wherever there is poverty, misery or financial disaster, you have power to bring the prosperity of the Kingdom.

How will you do it? By activating the power of the Holy Spirit. This means it will not be your words of human wisdom that will bring the sinner out of the life of sin, but the message that the Holy Spirit places in their hearts. The center of that message is Jesus Christ, and Him crucified (1 Corinthians 2: 2) and risen (Acts 17: 3). You have authority to demonstrate and bring to the natural world what Christ already gained on the cross. Anyone who is baptized with the Holy Spirit has the supernatural power of God and is authorized to manifest it.

> *The Lord never authorized the Church to preach the gospel without demonstrations of His miracles, signs and wonders.*

Wherever somebody preaches the gospel and there is no demonstration of power, that message lacks credibility. For what purpose is the gospel preached? It is to prove that Jesus Christ is alive and comes to seek His church; to confirm that the gospel of the Kingdom is truth; to remove man and woman from sin; to reconcile them with the Father, and to confront and subjugate Satan, thus reestablishing the defeat Jesus gave him on the cross.

3. Anoint us to do the impossible.

The anointing, given to every child of God thirsting for His presence, comes from baptism with the Holy Spirit, who is its steward. The Word shows us that *"... God anointed Jesus of Nazareth with the Holy Spirit and with power, who went about doing good and healing all who were oppressed by the devil, for God was with Him"* (Acts 10:38). In short, from the moment a believer receives baptism with the Holy Spirit, he or she is supernaturally empowered with divine ability to do the impossible.

> **The criteria that God uses to call someone to ministry is for that person to have been anointed with the Holy Spirit.**

Jesus was anointed and approved by the Father before beginning His ministry. This is confirmed in the book of Acts: *"Men of Israel, hear these words: Jesus of Nazareth, a Man attested by God to you by miracles, wonders, and signs which God did through Him in your midst, as you yourselves also know*" (Acts 2:22). Here the word "approved" means being certified or accredited to perform a task. It means that until you have been baptized with the Holy Spirit, you will not be approved, certified or anointed to demonstrate the miracles, signs and wonders that God can do through a human being. In other words, you will not be qualified to do the work of the ministry.

> *No one can be a witness of Jesus without being certified with the baptism of the Holy Spirit, who gives us power and anointing to prove our testimony.*

The divine ability that rests over the life of a Christian comes from the person and the power of the Holy Spirit. Just as God anointing Jesus to do the impossible, He also anoints every one of His sons and daughters, to work above the natural. That is why in Mark 9:23 Jesus tells us: "*...If you can believe, all things are possible to him who believes.*"

> *The moment you are baptized with the Holy Spirit, the impossible becomes possible; then the world believes.*

4. Being a credible witness of Jesus.

A witness is someone who has seen, heard and experienced something firsthand; one who can present evidence. A witness of Christ is a person who has experienced His power, and can produce supernatural evidence of the existence of a supernatural God. Jesus knew that it was not enough to say He was Son of God, but that He had to prove it with visible works because people were unbelieving.

In one occasion, Jesus said: *"Believe Me that I am in the Father and the Father in Me, or else believe Me for the sake of the works themselves"* (John 14:11). On another, He also said: *"...you shall receive power when the Holy Spirit has come upon you; and you shall be witnesses to Me in Jerusalem, and in all Judea and Samaria, and to the end of the earth"* (Acts 1:8).

All Christians are called to be witnesses of Christ, but not all are credible ones. For that we must prove what we say, with visible and tangible evidence. No matter how many degrees or diplomas a person has, if he cannot prove the power and authority of God over demons, diseases, and the works of the enemy, he cannot be an effective witness of Jesus Christ. The titles that endorse human knowledge are useless if the power of God does not accompany them.

In Colombia, South America, there is a ministry that is moving steadily forward, led by Pastor Steven, who has the following testimony: "My family and I met each week with a group of people in Medellin, Colombia, to worship God and Pray for the needs of the people. We are connected with King Jesus and Apostle Maldonado, and everything we receive from there we apply it here. We have been baptized with the Holy Spirit and His power, and now we are effective witnesses of Jesus. We are walking in an outpour of the glory of God and the signs are plenty. We see financial miracles, people free from demonic oppression, others are healed of serious illnesses, blind people now see or the previously deaf can hear.

"Since the Apostle began to impart God's power to us, we do not cease to grow. We now have prayer and evangelism groups throughout the city of Medellin. On one occasion, a pregnant woman asked us for prayer because she had been diagnosed with a brain tumor. When she returned to the doctor to run tests, the tumor had completely disappeared! But then, the doctor (the best specialist in the city) had a second set of news for her. He told her that her child had a serious problem with her heart, as well as Down Syndrome. The only option offered by medicine was abortion, the doctors confirmed that they could not do anything. In faith, she said she would not do that and continued to attend our meetings believing for a miracle.

"The girl's father, on the other hand, resigned himself and thought that their lives would change forever; that they would have to find a school for special children and dedicate themselves to taking care of the girl. But the wife said, 'I believe that God will perform a miracle.' In the prayer group, we spoke over the baby, canceled the medical diagnosis and declared, in the name of Jesus, that she would be born healthy. Three weeks before the birth, they tested the mother again and all showed good results. The doctor himself said: 'This cannot be! It's not the same girl I saw weeks ago.'

"Today, the girl's father also believes in God, gives Him glory and serves Him full of gratitude. This was possible because we are being continuously activated by our spiritual father, we are filled with the Holy Spirit, and we learned to walk in the supernatural."

God wants you to be a credible witness wherever you go. His desire is for you to work miracles, signs and wonders as Jesus did. If you have been baptized with the Holy Spirit, then take the next step; like Peter, when he got out of the boat and walked on the water with his eyes fixed on Jesus. Get out of the boat, and begin to take bold steps of faith. Demonstrate the power of God as you go through life, and the Holy Spirit will be with you!

THE NEED AND IMPORTANCE OF BEING BAPTIZED WITH THE HOLY SPIRIT

As I mentioned, the Church today does not give importance to being baptized with the Holy Spirit; it does not understand the necessity. Many in Church see ministry as something natural they can do it in their own strength, where they can flow with the currents of public opinion and adapt to the methods of the world. There are even leaders in the church who have emerged and prevailed thanks to their charisma and talent. They do not understand that the ministry is and should be supernatural, which can only be developed with the endorsement of God, and with the revelation and power of the Holy Spirit.

That is why it is common to see "burned out" believers, trying to serve God but completely exhausted. Many are hurt, beaten, tired, at the limits of their strength; and it is because they have struggled for years to do a supernatural task with their natural forces, without the help of the Holy Spirit.

Baptism with the Holy Spirit is essential to the growth of the Body of Jesus Christ. It is essential if we want to build the Church that Christ commanded us to. The baptism in Him is crucial to seeing changes and transformations of the heart, the ones that are supposed to happen every time a person receives the gospel and opens their heart to Jesus Christ.

Let us now see why it is important to receive and experience the baptism with the Holy Spirit:

1. Baptism in the Holy Spirit is a commandment, not an option.

We have seen that Jesus prepared His disciples by giving them clear indications of what they should do when He was no longer physically on the earth. They were not suggestions or options, but clear and precise mandates. They were orders that could not be ignored, otherwise they would fail on their commission.

That is why, *"being assembled together with them, He commanded them not to depart from Jerusalem, but to wait for the Promise of the Father..."* (Acts 1:4). Jesus knew that the baptism of the Holy Spirit was the only way His disciples could do, legally and effectively, what He had entrusted to them. Today, that mandate extends to all of us who have decided to follow Jesus, live the life He lived and establish His Kingdom on earth. The power of the Holy Spirit is the only one who overcomes Satan, and the authority of Jesus Christ is the only one he recognizes.

> **People think that baptism in the Holy Spirit is optional, because they see ministry as a professional career.**

What distinguishes the Church of Jesus Christ from any religion is that it worships a living God who is present among His people through His Holy Spirit. Thus, when we say that a church is a "house of God," we do not refer to a building where men gather, but to a place where He dwells and the power of His Holy Spirit manifests itself fully and continuously. Any other place where God is not present and His power is not manifested is more like a social club, where people come together to sing, entertain each other and waste time.

Jesus taught His disciples about the Holy Spirit, telling them to remain in Jerusalem and be baptized by Him. There they were invested with His power to fulfill the commission entrusted to them, having the Spirit of God as a guide and counselor. I honestly do not understand how people can say that they will accomplish what God called them to do, without being baptized with the Holy Spirit and His supernatural power.

I consider that there is much ignorance in the people of God about this subject. Many live by ministry like if it were a career; as would a lawyer, a doctor, a business administrator, and so on. There are many pastors who have graduated from universities, but who have not been forged in the presence of God, nor processed by the fire of the Holy Spirit. I agree that Christians should be intellectually prepared; our ministry encourages young people to study and we have worked hard to have our own university. However, I believe that the Word without revelation and without demonstration of the supernatural power of God is incomplete.

What I want to establish clearly is that if a Christian prepares theologically for pastoral ministry, but does not have the baptism of the Holy Spirit, his pastorate will be as lacking in the spirit as any other career. Jesus studied the Torah and the prophets much of His life; but what marked His calling, His anointing and His commission to the work of the ministry was the baptism with the Holy Spirit in the Jordan, and the voice of the Father who validated Him.

> *A biblical institute cannot give you faith, anointing or a calling; only the Lord can.*

Without baptism with the Holy Spirit, believers will be destined to be unproductive, for there is no way to bear fruit in our own strength, nor a way to fulfill what Jesus commissioned us. In turn, we become nothing but natural men and women, with no strength or power to confront Satan, or to overcome sin and our flesh. We will only win if we receive the baptism with the Holy Spirit.

2. The baptism with the Holy Spirit is a need.

Through the prophet Zachariah, the Lord gave His backing to Zerubbabel, David's descendant and Governor of Judah after the exile (Haggai 1:1), who had been sent to rebuild the temple in Jerusalem. He spoke to Him and said: *"This is the word of the Lord to Zerubbabel: 'Not by might nor by power, but by My Spirit,' Says the Lord of hosts"* (Zachariah 4:6).

God spoke to Zerubbabel because he had an important mission to fulfill and would face great spiritual opposition. Rebuilding the temple in Jerusalem represented much more than lifting its walls and restoring its former splendor. Reconstruction meant that God would once again be worshiped in Israel and that the people would have a new opportunity to remain pure before God, to be obedient to His voice and to become His chosen nation.

As with Zerubbabel, whenever we carry out the work of the ministry that God has entrusted to us, we need His power to overcome the opposition. The trials come through sin, the flesh, the impossible, the difficult circumstances of life and so many other traps that the devil places in our path. The power of His Spirit is the legal and effective means that the Lord provides us to be victorious in everything we do.

During my time in ministry, I have found great need in the body of Christ and in the world. Many people, both believers and unbelievers, are sick, bound to drugs, tormented and afflicted, and full of fears, suicidal tendencies, bitterness, unforgiveness, loneliness, and broken hearts. In addition, I have found countless young people who do not know what direction to take in life. Evil, perversion, and decadence are advancing by leaps and bounds.

However, nothing can be resolved with natural weapons. Only the power of God will be able to destroy the works of the devil and supply the needs of the people, because it's written that, *"... the yoke will be destroyed because of the anointing ..."* (Isaiah 10:27).

It really surprises me to see so many people giving counseling today, when what is needed is a higher power. I believe in counseling; in fact, I have a doctorate in Counseling, however, I know that you can only advise a person who is in sound mind or emotionally stable. So, what should we do with the depressed, the suicidal, the drug-bound, those on the verge of divorce or fearing losing their children? A pill does not solve the problem, nor does a well-intentioned advice solve a crisis.

Before following any advice, these people need to be free from the evil power that binds them, from the generational curses, from the demons that subjugate certain areas of their life. To be free from the selfishness that destroys their homes and their generations, they need to know the Fatherhood of God and receive His supernatural love. The only person I know, capable of bringing peace, conviction, comfort, guidance, revelation and manifesting the power of God, is the Holy Spirit.

We need the Holy Spirit to know the root of any problem. Counseling deals with the branches of a problem, with the consequences and external expressions of something that at first sight is not noticed, but whose root we hardly arrived at. That is why, in order to minister to others, we need the Holy Spirit's guidance, and in turn, people themselves need to be filled with the Spirit to deal with their problems effectively, from the inside out.

3. Baptism with the Holy Spirit is the original activation in the supernatural realm.

When we are baptized with the Holy Spirit, we have the ability to bind everything on earth from the devil and from the curse of sin because it is already forbidden in the heavens. In addition, we can declare on earth that God's will be done, just as it is done in heaven. There is no depression in heaven, and there should not be any here either; there is no cancer in heaven, there must be no disease on earth. It means that if we encounter a depressed person, we can bind the depression in the name of Jesus, and release peace, faith, joy and God's love over it. Likewise, if we find a person dying because of the cancer that afflicts their body, we can bind the spirits of sickness and death, and release the whole work of Christ on the cross for that person to be healed.

Pastor George from Ghana—a country in West Africa—knows what it is to be activated in the supernatural realm. He came to our ministry as a member of a Presbyterian church and the first time he attended our annual conference, he was impacted by supernatural manifestations of God's power. That motivated him to return to one of our training schools for leaders to be activated in the supernatural power of God. Here is his testimony:

"Apostle Maldonado prophesied to us, saying that God would send us to begin a new ministry; and that is what we did when we returned, filled with the Holy Spirit. Since then, we have seen the power of God healing people with HIV, cancer, epilepsy and many other diseases that doctors say are incurable. Recently, a lady with a gangrenous foot came to our church. Since she had no money and could not afford the hospital, she was sent back home. We went to see her and prayed for her for ten days in a row, until the power of God worked in her and she was completely healed.

"Another miracle took place with an eighteen-year-old boy who went to the hospital with a severe stomach ache. The doctor told him that he had a hernia and prescribed a medicine for the discomfort. Two days later he returned because he could not bear the pain. This time, they did another study and discovered that he had a torn testicle. The doctors told him that he needed urgent surgery because, after six hours, the testicle could become dark from lack of blood and die, so the only solution was to remove it.

"Before the operation, the young man came to me and we prayed, and then returned to the hospital. When the doctors prepared to remove the testicle—since according to them it was already dead—they realized that the testicle regained its normal color. They had never seen that before, so they decided to stop the procedure and watch what happened. By the next 25 minutes, the dead testicle came back to life. The power of God healed it! The surgeons closed the wound and sent the boy home."

Since being activated and empowered by the Holy Spirit, Pastor George walks in the supernatural power of God, demonstrating it through miracles, signs and wonders.

HOW TO RECEIVE THE BAPTISM WITH THE HOLY SPIRIT AND POWER

As I pointed out at the beginning, the purpose for which the Spirit of God guided me to write this book is that each reader comes to live the experience of being baptized with Him. I pray that every word written here will be imbued with the presence of the Spirit, release the supernatural power of God, and that He will come upon you. Remember that this is a promise of the Father from the Old Testament. It is something that He longs to give, so do not despise Him or let yourself feel unworthy, to the extent of rejecting Him. Do not think that His presence is for others and not for you, that it is for another time, or that it must be in a special situation. Today is the day, this is the time and the moment to receive Him. Just open your heart.

Baptism with the Holy Spirit is received in many ways:

1. By faith.

Apostle Paul said: *"Therefore He who supplies the Spirit to you and works miracles among you, does He do it by the works of the law, or by the hearing of faith?"* (Galatians 3:5). In the same way that we received salvation when we went to the altar and believed that Jesus Christ is the Son of God, so we also receive the Holy Spirit today: by faith.

Jesus said that God the Father will give us the Holy Spirit if we ask Him. *"If a son asks for bread from any father among you, will he give him a stone? Or if he asks for a fish, will he give him a serpent instead of a fish?"* (Luke 11:13). When you received Jesus in your heart, you had to take a step of faith, to believe in something that was not yet in you. That faith is a gift of God for salvation. So, it is also when we receive the Holy Spirit; you do not see Him, but believe by faith and receive His power.

The Father longs to pour His Spirit upon us again. Since Adam departed from the presence of God, the Father forged a plan of redemption at a very high cost. The goal is for us to become part of His family again; to put back His Spirit in us and give us the supernatural abilities that were taken away from us when our spirit died because of sin. Today we cannot see how Adam saw, but faith gives us that ability to see in the spiritual world. That faith is what makes it possible for us to receive the Spirit of God.

2. By spiritual hunger and thirst.

Jesus said: *"He who believes in Me, as the Scripture has said, out of his heart will flow rivers of living water.' But this He spoke concerning the Spirit, whom those believing in Him would receive"* (John 7:38-39). How much do you want to receive from the Holy Spirit? Are you content with 10 percent, 50 percent, or do you want it all? Do you want to be immersed in that miraculous power of God, to be saturated in it? If you want to, the Holy Spirit will come upon you and baptize you with power from on high. He is drawn to those who are thirsty and hungry for Him.

> *Hunger precedes satiety; thirst precedes fullness.*

"Blessed are you who hunger now, for you shall be filled." (Luke 6:21). Thirst increases the ability to drink and hunger increases the ability to ingest food. So it is with our spirit. God cannot fill you beyond your capacity for satisfaction. If you are happy just reading the Bible as a history book, if you are happy with a traditional Christianity, you will not want any more, and you will not receive the baptism with the Holy Spirit. But if you want more, if you are hungry and thirsty for the Holy Spirit and want to be used with power to be a witness of Christ, then you will be submerged and baptized

with the Holy Spirit and receive His power to do great works.

> *Everyone who hungers and thirsts for the Holy Spirit will be sated with His supernatural baptism.*

3. The Spirit gives you tongues, but you must speak them.

Many people want to be baptized with the Holy Spirit, with the evidence of speaking in other tongues, but they think the Holy Spirit will move their mouths for them, and that is not how it works. The Spirit gives us the gift of tongues, but we must speak them. The problem is people begin to reason and figure out what they are going to say. But reason cannot dictate what to say in tongues, for what one speaks will proceed from his spirit; that is, from the depths of his inner being.

My advice is that you begin to open your mouth, worshiping God in your language. Do not plan what you are going to say; instead let the words of flow from your heart. You can say, "Lord, I adore You, I exalt Your name and I receive Your Holy Spirit." As you worship God, almost without realizing it, the Holy Spirit will take control of your tongue and you will begin to speak a heavenly language.

Another recommendation is that you do not attempt to speak everything at once. It often begins with one or two words. Other times it comes as a babble of words, but as you continue to speak, your vocabulary is filled with heavenly tongues. Remember that you might not receive the gift of interpreting tongues nor the gift of speaking various kinds of tongues; but the evidence of having received the baptism with the Holy Spirit is to speak tongues of the Spirit.

> *Jesus, our role model to living empowered by the Spirit.*

From the time He came to earth, until He ascended to heaven, Jesus Christ was one hundred percent God and one hundred percent man. Jesus, the Son of God, had to shed His robe of glory to live among us. From His birth to His resurrection and ascension into heaven, the Holy Spirit was enveloped in every aspect of His earthly life. As a man, He modeled to us how to live, always in communion with His Father and obeying Him in everything.

Jesus lived on earth as a man led by the Holy Spirit, not as God. The Holy Spirit received His robe of anointing, His power to perform miracles, the revelation of who He was and His purpose on earth. His example teaches us to depend on the Holy Spirit and to demonstrate and manifest the kingdom of God on earth. We all have the same potential to be born of the Spirit, to be empowered and used by Him, as Jesus Christ was. What did Jesus do as a man? He completely surrendered His will, thus qualifying for the Holy Spirit to dwell in Him without measure.

The question is: do you have the same right as Christ to be used by God? The answer is yes. We all do because Christ won it for us on the cross of Calvary. That is why He sent the Holy Spirit to empower us. God never gives us the limited Holy Spirit. Instead, once He comes upon us, the responsibility is ours, and it is up to us to act fully and without measure.

> **The will of God is unlimited in you, just as it was in Jesus, thanks to the Holy Spirit.**

The Holy Spirit worked without measure inside Jesus, empowering Him and anointing Him to perform great works, "which if they were written one by one, I suppose that even the world itself could not contain the books that would be written" (John 21:25). Jesus walked on water, opened the eyes of the blind, raised the dead, gave life to a dry hand, cured the paralyzed, turned water into wine, cursed a fig tree that did not bear fruit and it dried; He set free those oppressed by the devil, caused the deaf to speak and be heard, multiplied the loaves and fishes, fed crowds, drew money from the mouth of a fish, and calmed a storm. He prophesied, brought sinners to repentance, was transfigured on the mountain while praying with His disciples, gave His life to save mankind, and rose again on the third day as it had been prophesied.

He did all this with the power and strength of the Spirit of God, and anyone who receives the baptism with the Holy Spirit has the same potential to do this and more, because He promised that: *"…He who believes in Me, the works that I do he will do also; and greater works than these he will do, because I go to My Father"* (John 14:12).

POWER AND AUTHORITY ARE AVAILABLE TO EVERY BELIEVER

Traditional teachings have tried to convince us that we must have a special anointing for God to use us supernaturally, to heal the sick, to preach the gospel of the Kingdom, to speak in tongues or to have a ministry on earth. However, the Scripture teaches us that when Jesus sent out His seventy disciples He did it in a simple way, saying: *"Whatever city you enter, and they receive you, eat such things as are set before you. And heal the sick there, and say to them: The kingdom of God has come near to you"* (Luke 10:8-9).

According to Mark, the only requirement is to believe and do so in the name of Jesus: *"And He said to them: Go into all the world and preach the gospel to every creature. [...] And these signs will follow those who believe. In My name they will cast out demons; they will speak with new tongues; they will take up serpents; and if they drink anything deadly, it will by no means hurt them; they will lay hands on the sick, and they will recover"* (Mark 16:15, 17-18).

The Holy Spirit is not for a chosen few. All who believe, all the children of God have the same universal call, which is to preach the Gospel of the Kingdom to every creature, and make disciples. We have all been promised the power to fulfill that commission, to prove that we are true witnesses. You can do the same things that Christ did. You are not bound, because the same Spirit that was in Jesus over two thousand years ago is the one dwelling in you today. Thanks to the Holy Spirit, we have the same capacity as Christ; otherwise, we would never reach His stature.

On one of my most recent trips to Mumbai, India, I met a 23-year-old youth named Paramjeet who had a meeting with the Holy Spirit and now lives passionately for God. In his own words, he testifies:

"I grew up with a Hindu and Sikh religious background, so every day of the week I worshiped a different god. I spent hours repeating mantras, and made long pilgrimages with idols upon my shoulders every three months. When I was ten years old I got into alcohol, cigarettes and drugs. As an adult, I came to have a business and a girlfriend, but I lost everything because of my lifestyle. Trying to get my company back, I got caught up in illegal business. Faced with the danger of being arrested, I tried to commit suicide several times; the last time I was on top of a seven-story building, ready to throw myself. But while I gathered the courage to jump, an old friend called me to invite me to his house, and I went.

"As soon as I entered, I was introduced to a man who was visiting, and he began to describe the condition of my life and introduced me to Jesus. The impact was such that I surrendered to the Lord that night. In four days my life changed completely, but I wanted more of God. Then I learned that in my city there would be a conference; 'Pray for India', where Apostle Maldonado would be present. I did not know him, but I saw an ad that read, 'Supernatural Encounter', which grabbed my attention and I went. At that moment, I knew I would meet God, face to face. On the third day of the event, the Apostle said: 'The glory of God is here; He is here; His Holy Spirit is upon you.' Next thing I knew, I was lying on the floor crying to God, when His Spirit came upon me, and I could see the face of Jesus and hear His voice.

"Those were the thirty most supernatural seconds I've ever lived. In addition, I experienced a creative miracle. I had injured my left forearm by accident one day, playing soccer on a prominent team in my country. As a result, I spent four hours in surgery, where two metal plates and thirteen screws were inserted in my arm. The doctor ruled that I could never lift anything heavy again. On the second day of the conference, during the ministration of miracles, the two plates and the thirteen screws became bones, by the power of God! That encounter, and seeing the power of God in my body, activated me to walk in the supernatural.

"When I left, I ran into a man walking on crutches, and I asked him, 'Would you like to walk without crutches?' He said yes so I prayed for him, and God healed him instantly! After that day, I have had many visitations and encounters with the Holy Spirit. He has led me to see the invisible; to intimacy with the Lord and has revealed my call. Since then, in less than a year, I have seen more than a hundred creative miracles: debts canceled, supernatural appearance of money, multiplication of food, new organs in the body of sick people, blind people who now see, bones healed and much, much more.

"God is using me in different countries of my region to teach and impart passion and true intimacy with Him, encounters with the Holy Spirit, and how to walk in the supernatural. The power of the Spirit is present to make miracles, signs and wonders in every place I go. I will always be grateful to have been imparted with the Holy

Spirit and His power. That passion for God and for the supernatural is renewed every day in me, because the Holy Spirit continually fills me."

> *He who is born of the Spirit lives in a state of innocence, and loses the appetite for sin.*

When Jesus was baptized in the Jordan, the heavens opened over Him as man, but on the day of Pentecost, as God, He opened a portal for all generations to come. That is why the Bible affirms that Jesus is the way and the truth. The Holy Spirit came first upon Jesus; and thanks to what He did with His power, today He can come upon us. All that the Son of God did was by and through the Holy Spirit, so that all who came behind Him could do the same.

Jesus was clothed in the uniform of anointing when He was baptized in the Jordan. As a result, the devil was upset and tried to challenge Him in every possible way, but as always, he ended up running away. The Spirit comes upon us and clothes us in the uniform of God, granting us His authority. Satan recognizes that uniform and that authority; that's why he submits.

Authority is the position from which we exercise the power that Jesus delegated to us. Outside of that position, it is illegal to use it. If we lead ourselves by biblical qualifications for ministry, many who are now leading churches, many who preach from a pulpit or pastor a congregation, would be disqualified.

If you want to preach the gospel of the Kingdom that Jesus commanded us to proclaim, with the manifestation of signs that He promised us, you need a fresh encounter with the Holy Spirit. Do you want to start today? Refuse to continue preaching a dead gospel, and grab on to the Holy Spirit until you are filled and baptized by Him. Only then will you become a legal and effective witness. Without the fullness and baptism of the Holy Spirit, we are dry and spiritually dead, for He alone reveals Jesus Christ and empowers us to be His witnesses on earth.

An example of this is provided by Pastors Shekhar and Lavina Kallianpur, founders of Global Worship Center in Mumbai, India. Their ministry is experiencing a radical change after being activated in the supernatural, and the testimonies of what the power of the Holy Spirit is doing in their country are shocking. Know their testimony:

"Ever since we got connected with Apostle Maldonado our life changed radically. I have been a pastor for 30 years, but after receiving the impartation of the supernatural, our ministry has gone to new dimensions! Now we see how Mumbai and the country are being transformed. I have witnessed the acceleration of the supernatural through signs, miracles and wonders. The blind see, the lame walk, and over the last two years, the dead have risen on three different occasions.

"One day during a miracle crusade, a pregnant woman came, whose water bag had been broken in the womb, and the baby's heartbeat disappeared. According to the doctors, the child died in the womb, but she believed God by a miracle. A week later, doctors found that the water bag had been refilled and the baby was resurrected!

"Another powerful testimony is that of a woman from another city, who had been declared brain dead and bedridden. We came together and prayed for her by telephone, in the name of Jesus. When we finished praying, she began to walk!

"We now have spiritual children in various cities. For example, in Bangalore there is a pastor who is a doctor. We recently prayed for him and gave him what we have received from God. Today, this man prays, puts his hands on terminally-ill patients and they are healed. After the pastor prayed for him, a child who had been diagnosed with brain death, came back to life!"

When you are born again, your character, your nature and your heart change. That is our first contact with the

> *If someone has not been baptized with the Holy Spirit, they are incapable of proving that what they preach is true.*

Spirit, where we receive His breath of eternal life. Now you need the second experience, which is to be baptized with Him.

Activation Prayer

Dear friend, if you have not received the baptism with the Holy Spirit until now, with the evidence of speaking in heavenly tongues, repeat this prayer with me, with a loud voice and with all your faith:

> *"Heavenly Father, Your Word says that if men know how to give good gifts to their children, how much more will You, as my Father, give me the promise of the Spirit! Therefore, as Your son, washed by the blood of Christ, born again, knowing that my name is written in the book of life and that I have eternal life, I ask You to give me the experience of being baptized with Your Spirit. I make a commitment to be a faithful and legal witness on earth, to preach Christ in time and out of time with Your supernatural power. Heavenly Father, fill me and baptize me today with the Holy Spirit and power.*
>
> *I want to use that power over the enemy, over sickness, over nature, over oppression, to heal the sick, to raise the dead and to destroy the works of the devil. Heavenly Father, I believe that at the very moment of being baptized, I will be authorized to demonstrate Your power on earth, just as Jesus did, as the apostles did, and as all the men and women You have raised in*

the earth. Lord, through this baptism, I declare that I am anointed to do the impossible. Anoint me to be a credible witness. Wherever I go, I will carry Your gospel with power, miracles, signs and wonders. Fill me and baptize me with Your Holy Spirit. I receive it in the name of Jesus. Holy Spirit fill me now. Amen."

If you repeated this prayer, right there where you are, start speaking in another language. Receive this impartation now as you read this book!

Lord, I pray that the person who is reading this book will be filled and baptized with the Holy Spirit, and empowered to serve You effectively. I declare they are enabled to consecrate themselves to Jesus Christ and to carry out Your purpose on earth. Holy Spirit of God, fill every reader with power and authority to heal the sick, raise the dead, free captives, and preach the gospel with power. Fill them to be credible witnesses of Jesus Christ.

Beloved reader, if you are already a believer and have been baptized with the Holy Spirit, but long for a fresh filling of the Spirit of God, receive it also. Start speaking in new languages, now! I declare that everything that was asleep or dead in you awakens and comes alive. I rebuke every spirit of religiosity and spiritual death, and declare the life of the Spirit in you, now, in the name of Jesus!

If you know other Christians who have lost the fire for God and need to rekindle it, give them freely what you have received today by grace. From this moment, wherever you go, walk with freedom and courage. Preach the gospel of the kingdom, teach the Word with demonstrations of the power of God, and destroy the works of the devil, because you are authorized by Jesus Christ to do it. Amen!

3

The Outpouring of the Holy Spirit in the End Times

The Holy Spirit has participated in the great events of humanity, and is present every time the Father wants to bring something new to the earth or to a generation. Like everything God does, the outpours of the Holy Spirit do not happen without a reason, but are determined by times and seasons. There is no way to recognize the seasons or the kind of outpouring that is or will be happening, unless we are connected to the Spirit of God and follow the direction of His currents and waves.

In the Scriptures, we see the Holy Spirit participating in the opening of new spiritual portals, events which the Word calls "open heavens." In Ezekiel 1:1, the prophet testifies to having had the privilege of living this experience. Since then and until our time, the longing of God's people is that He breaks the heavens and descends so that we may see His presence (Isaiah 64:1). That is why, wherever there is an outpouring of the Holy Spirit, it is because the heavens are open over that place, and vice versa.

In the times we live, everything is being shaken. This is the most explosive era when it comes to information and technology, where so much is available to us at the touch of a button; and nearly everything is faster and more comfortable. The greatest discoveries in science and technology have been made in recent centuries, but there are still issues that man cannot solve. That is why the Bible says: *"And there will be strange signs in the sun, moon, and stars. And here on earth the nations will be in turmoil, perplexed by the roaring seas and strange tides"* (Luke 21:25 – NTV).

The "perplexed" word in the verse above means *no way out, dubious, uncertain,* and *confused.* There are chaotic situations that man cannot overcome; events he will not know how to react to, and which will keep him confused. For example, we do not find solutions to the conflict between Israel and Palestine, the Middle East crisis, the disaster of the world economy, the endless incurable diseases, the intense persecution of the Church in the world or the worsening climate imbalances.

The rulers of the earth have no solution for this; no matter what they try, no one can provide the right answer. As a result, people are discouraged and perplexed. They are unsatisfied or have become hopeless because they expect something which has not happened. The only remedy against discouragement and perplexity is the outpouring of the Holy Spirit.

THE BEGINNING OF THE HOLY SPIRIT'S OUTPOURING

When the Day of Pentecost had fully come, they were all with one accord in one place. And suddenly there came a sound from heaven, as of a rushing mighty wind, and it filled the whole house where they were sitting. Then there appeared to them divided tongues, as of fire, and one sat upon each of them. And they were all filled with the Holy Spirit and began to speak with other tongues, as the Spirit gave them utterance...

(ACTS 2:1-4)

Pentecost is a Greek word meaning "fifty". Historically it is associated with the Feast of Harvest, a celebration that was celebrated 50 days after Easter, in which God was praised for the fruits of the harvest. It was during Pentecost—50 days after the Resurrection of Jesus Christ—that the outpouring of His Spirit began over the earth. Since then and over the centuries, it has not ceased to spread.

> When a glass is filled to overflow, what is inside flows out. If we have been filled with the Holy Spirit, we should expect the outpouring.

When the Holy Spirit came upon the apostles gathered in the upper room, they were clothed with the anointing and power of God to fulfill the commission that Jesus had given them. Today we continue to live in His perfect timing and, as promised, we are at the gates of the greatest harvest of souls in history, which will come through an outpouring of the Spirit in areas like evangelism, discipleship, Houses of Peace, social aid organizations, and many more.

In the Bible, we see that the feasts of the Lord mark the beginning of a new season. Thus, when we want to calculate the time where an event prophesied in Scripture will occur, the feasts are the most precise guides. For example, a question everyone asks is, "When will the second coming of the Lord be"? Jesus said no one knows this (Matthew 25:13). However, He gave us signs pointing to the feast of Pentecost and the outpouring of the Spirit.

According to the Hebrew calendar, this feast lasts for two days. Through prophet Hosea, the Lord promised that, *"After two days He will revive us; on the third day He will raise us up, that we may live in His sight"* (Hosea

6:2). As for those "two days", apostle Peter wrote: *"But, beloved, do not forget this one thing, that with the Lord one day is as a thousand years, and a thousand years as one day"* (2 Peter 3:8). Here we see that a day for God is like a thousand years for us, and a thousand years of ours are a day for God, so the Bible says it will last two days. This means we are living the end of the feast right now.

I said before that the feasts of God are precise; they are His watch and calendar to identify the times that we live. Where are we now in God's time? Many make the mistake of counting the two thousand years since the birth of Jesus; but the feast of Pentecost began when the Holy Spirit came upon the disciples in the upper room. Jesus was born around the year 4 BC. And died when He was about thirty-three, in 29 AD; He rose again on the third day and stayed another forty days with the disciples, teaching them about the Kingdom. Then He rose into heaven and told them to wait for the coming of the Holy Spirit. If that is accurate, 1988 years have passed since the Spirit of God came upon the disciples of Jesus.

In the Roman (Gregorian) calendar we are in 2017, but if we lead ourselves by the Feasts of the Lord we have not yet reached 2000 years. In addition, we know that the calendar has changed about three times in 20 centuries. First was the Egyptian Calendar, then the Julian and finally the Gregorian. According to this, there are 12 years left till the end of the holidays; so the two thousand years, or the two days spoken of by the prophet Hosea, are yet to be fulfilled.

With this, I do not intend to establish when exactly the second coming of the Lord will be because, *"Of that day and hour no one knows, not even the angels in heaven, nor the Son, but only the Father"* (Mark 13:32); But we can recognize the signs and discern the seasons. This outpouring of the Holy Spirit tells us that it is time to be ready for the second coming of Jesus. Before He comes, the Church will witness the greatest outpouring of the Holy Spirit ever seen on earth. So, do not think, as some people do, that there is plenty of time. I think we have very little left! The Lord's time is coming and we must be prepared!

Knowing this, your local church must be continually experiencing the mighty move of the Holy Spirit. There is an outpouring and overflow of His anointing falling on every continent and nation. In South America, Asia, Central America, the United States, Australia, Europe, Africa, and on all women, men, young people, the elderly and children. The same must be happening in your congregation!

The Scriptures give us another sign indicating the fulfillment of the times, by saying that the end of the feast will be marked by a judgment. *"For the time has come for judgment to begin at the house of God; and if it begins with us first, what will be the end of those who do not obey* the gospel of God?" (1 Peter 4:17). The feast of Pentecost began with grace, but will end with judgment; and it will start with us. That is why we need to warn everyone against sin and give priority to the message of holiness through the Holy Spirit. He is holy, and imparts to us holiness to empower us against sin.

> We must judge ourselves not to be judged by God. Repent of your sins!

THE OUTPOURING OF THE HOLY SPIRIT

What is the outpouring of the Holy Spirit? It is a supernatural activity of the Spirit of God in response to the promise of the Father. In the Old Testament God said: *"And it shall come to pass afterward that I will pour out My Spirit on all flesh; your sons and your daughters shall prophesy, your old men shall dream dreams, your young men shall see visions"* (Joel 2:28). Therefore, if someone says that he has an outpouring of the Holy Spirit, but nothing supernatural occurs in his life, he is lying or does not know what an outpouring is. God also promised, *"For I will pour water on him who is thirsty, and floods on the dry ground; I will pour My Spirit on your descendants, and My blessing on your offspring"* (Isaiah 44:3).

The outpouring of the Holy Spirit was spoken of by the prophets of the Old Testament and began to be fulfilled on the day of Pentecost in Jerusalem (Acts 2). An outpouring occurs because of the excess accumulation of a liquid in a vessel, which overflows once it reaches the vessel's limit. In the Bible, the word outpouring appears tied to elements such as early and late rain, first and last glory, and others.

The outpouring of the Spirit is always accompanied by the distribution of spiritual gifts, as well as the demonstration of the power of God. According to the biblical text, the true outpouring of the Holy Spirit will occur when Christ returns a second time (Zechariah 12:10). It means that the outpouring of the Spirit we see is a reminder of God's promise. That is supported in Deuteronomy 28:2 when Moses said that blessings will overtake us.

> *A true outpouring is an uncontrollable explosion that defeats human understanding.*

The outpouring of the Holy Spirit is also the evidence of the resurrection of Jesus Christ in the now, as it proves that He is alive today. This is a very important revelation because if we deny the outpouring of the Spirit, we are implicitly also denying the resurrection of the Son of God.

There are several ways of referring to the outpouring of the Holy Spirit; among them, the following:

- **Revival**

    This means to return to life something that was dead. The Church was born in the middle of an outpouring; That is its original state or environment. The early Christians moved in the power of the Spirit, manifesting miracles, signs and wonders, because they were "revived" by the Spirit of God. Thus, any church that does not have manifestations of the Spirit of God today needs a revival.

- **Visitation from God**

    A divine visitation occurs when God presents Himself to an individual or group, in one of His different manifestations. For example, as a provider, healer, deliverer, or Father. From the beginning, God has wanted not only to visit us, but to dwell or have an abode in each one of us and in His church.

> In the times we live, all of us need a visitation from God in the now.

There are two types of visitation: the first is sovereign and initiated by God Himself, according to His divine will. This obeys the fulfillment of the plans He has for His children and for the whole earth in this season. The second type of visitation is provoked, and it occurs by the collective hunger of the people, which arises by the grace of the Holy Spirit in their hearts. This yearning is born in the people for diverse reasons. For example, injustices, poverty, disease, death, etc. Hunger causes a cry in the people and puts a demand on God so that His mighty hand may move on their behalf. When that cry of the people rises to the presence of God, He sends an outpouring of His Spirit in response. However, it is important to know that a visitation from God may be different for each of us; Therefore, we must be attentive, discern, hear His voice and obey.

> No one can say he has experienced a visitation from the Lord if he did not hear the voice of God.

When we do not discern the time of His visitation, we cannot prepare for it. It takes us by surprise and we suffer the consequences of God's judgment. The judgment results in the Spirit of God lifting from a person, city or nation; the manifestation of the supernatural stops, and our lives and ministries go through a period of dryness.

Jerusalem did not recognize the time of its visitation. That is why the Scriptures say, *"Now as He drew near, He saw the city and wept over it, saying: If you had known, even you, especially in this your day, the things that make for your peace! But now they are hidden from your eyes. For days will come upon you when your enemies will build an embankment around you, surround you and close you in on every side, and level you, and your children within you, to the ground; and they will not leave in you one stone upon another, because you did not know the time of your visitation"* (Luke 19:41-44).

Why did Jerusalem fail to recognize the time of His visitation? Years before, the nation had removed the school of prophets, which kept it aware of the things the Spirit of God was doing. Instead it only kept the synagogues, which were teaching and discussion groups, where the Spirit of the Lord did not move. The prophets bring the voice, the word and the revelation of God. However, today the prophetic voice has been silenced, and many don't realize that, *"...Surely the Lord God does nothing, unless He reveals His secret to His servants the prophets"* (Amos 3:7).

■ A spiritual awakening

A spiritual awakening refers to reviving or mobilizing a large group of people, just as it was when the time came for God to restore Jerusalem, after seventy years in exile. "So the Lord stirred up the spirit of

Zerubbabel the son of Shealtiel, governor of Judah, and the spirit of Joshua the son of Jehozadak, the high priest, and the spirit of all the remnant of the people; and they came and worked on the house of the Lord of hosts, their God" (Haggai 1:14).

Each outpouring, revival and visitation produces a spiritual awakening. All our nations, cities and countries desperately need one! *"Repent therefore and be converted, that your sins may be blotted out, so that times of refreshing may come from the presence of the Lord, and that He may send Jesus Christ, who was preached to you before"* (Acts 3:19-20). To be "converted" is to change form, to leave a shape behind and move on to a new one. When the Word says that our sins must be "blotted out," it means that they must be completely removed from memory; and for that we must repent.

> **The less sin we have, the greater weight of God's presence we can bear.**

If we repent and convert, then times of refreshment will come, which manifest as a season of rest. Before the Lord returns, the Church must rest from all kinds of evil. To rest in God is to release the burdens that weigh us down and surrender completely, trusting fully in Him. The times of refreshment precede the coming of the Lord; as such the outpouring of the Spirit is a sign of the end times.

- **Spiritual movement**

    In the past, we have seen many movements in America and the world. In the first decade of the twentieth century, revival occurred on Azusa Street in Los Angeles, California (USA). Then came the Voice of Healing in the '40s. The Discipleship movement was seen in the '60s. In the '70s came the movement of the Word. In the '80 the Prophetic movement. In the '90s the Apostolic movement.

At the beginning of the year 2000, the movements finished and the celebrities arose, where a single person with a gift was given prominence, and it was assumed that only he or she could be used to manifest the power of God. This must change. The movement is about God, not the gifts of men. We are in a time where we must cry out to enter into a spiritual awakening as individuals, ministries and the body of Christ. We need this to manifest in our lives.

> *A movement is a thought of God in action.*

To understand the movement of Spirit, let us compare it with the waters of a river. Often, we see deep waters that have no movement. Likewise, there are people who speak very deeply, but do not produce a spiritual movement.

There is a great different between a movement and a gift:

- The gift of rhetoric does not replace the presence of the Spirit of God.

- Movement is an action that God provokes in His sovereignty. The gift is a divine grace by which the will of man operates.

- All movements occur around God, and although the gift also comes from God, it works around man and his personality.

- The movement leaves a legacy behind, but the gift does not because gifts cannot be imparted.

- The gift dies when the man who carries it dies. However, the movement passes from one generation to another.

About this I can share my own testimony. For twenty years, I have trained thousands of spiritual sons and daughters in churches and ministries around the world, and they all end up moving in the same realms of the supernatural where I move. This happens because a spiritual movement does not cease to advance and grow, and these are some of the characteristics that define it. It is not the gift of a person trying to do something alone, but a whole generation impacted and revived by the

Spirit of God. In the end, all reproduce not my model, but the model of the Kingdom.

I recently returned from an apostolic trip to various countries in Africa. In Ethiopia, I ministered to millions of people with the Word and power of God. When I called for those who wanted to receive the baptism with the Holy Spirit and power, more than one million people received it in an instant and were activated to walk in the supernatural!

In the city of Hyderabad, India, there is a girl named Vandana, who has a shocking testimony I want to share with you:

"When I was four, one night I woke up with severe nasal bleeding; I was taken to the hospital and the doctors diagnosed me with a genetic disorder called hemophilia. That meant that my blood's ability to coagulate was very weak. This led me to bleed severely before the smallest wound. That disease has no cure, so I lived through the next 23 years facing the risk of imminent death. I would bleed from the ears, eyes, mouth and gums, and sometimes vomited blood. About ten days a month I would spend hospitalized, medicated, and connected to respirators and oxygen masks. I was suffering from seeing large clots of blood coming out of my female parts or accumulating in my lungs. Every year I had to receive blood transfusions to control both the external bleeding and the internal bleeding.

"My family was very affected. My father had to retire from work and was the one who donated blood for my transfusions. Soon, medical bills became a financial burden for my family. Because of the instability of my life, I had no friends, and I could not go to school or have a relationship. Since I was allergic to painkillers, I cried every night in pain and I had no hope that this would end. The only way out was death. One night, I began to feel severe stomach pains. When I went to the doctor, he found cancerous cysts in me. I stayed bedridden for two months in my house, but the treatments did not work, so I began begging my father to take me to a Hindu prayer place to seek my healing. My parents called an ambulance and we started looking for a hospital to receive me; However, they refused to enter because I was at level VII of hemophilia, which is the final stage, and I only expected death.

"Not knowing what else to do, I called a friend and told her what was going on. She told me that she would come to my house to pray for me. When she arrived, she told me about the television show "The Supernatural Now" from Apostle Maldonado, and told me that even if the doctors could not do anything, the Holy Spirit was going to come to me and Jesus was going to heal me. My friend began to pray for me and I began to tremble. My whole body shook! She prayed for about fifteen minutes in the tongues of the Spirit. At that moment, my father came into my room, saw what was happening and began to defy God saying, 'If that God is real, then He heals you now'. To his surprise, when my friend finished praying, I got out of bed and stood by myself! I touched my stomach and the pain was gone! That day, I was able to eat, walk, and sit without pain and without bleeding. In an instant, the Holy Spirit touched me and I was baptized into Him. The glory of God filled my being and my body was healthy.

"My father called the whole family and they all saw the miracle happen before their eyes, and gave glory to God! From that encounter, my life changed. I come from a Hindu and Orthodox family, and used to hate Christians, but now I have a new life. The bleeding stopped and I no longer feel alone or depressed. The doctors did not find any trace of hemophilia in my body again. Now, I have daily encounters with the Holy Spirit."

THE NATURE AND CHARACTER OF AN OUTPOURING OF THE SPIRIT

I believe that it is important for every believer to recognize the nature and character of an outpouring. This is the only way to discern and capture it in his spirit, follow His waves and currents, and not lose His blessings. The outpouring of the Spirit is:

- **Indescribable**

    "But as it is written: 'Eye has not seen, nor ear heard, nor have entered into the heart of man the things

which God has prepared for those who love Him.' But God has revealed them to us through His Spirit. For the Spirit searches all things, yes, the deep things of God." (1 CORINTHIANS 2:9-10)

The outpouring manifests itself in many ways and extends to levels we cannot understand or describe. It takes years to appreciate the dimension and impact of an overflow of God.

■ Outside our control

The outpouring surpasses our reason, control and doctrine. Because of this, it is often resisted sine people are afraid to let go and lose control of their lives and ministry. The outpour is not something that can be handled. When the Spirit comes, there is no doctrine of man nor customs, rules or regulations that can box it in; instead He flows everywhere He is discerned and received, firmly tied to the will of God.

■ Spontaneous, sudden and explosive

One of the words that best describes the overflow produced by the Spirit is "bubbling". In this case, the nature of the outpouring is not a calm or controlled stream, as when pouring a glass of water. Instead it is sudden, explosive and unpredictable, as when the water boils, making noise.

The outpouring of the Spirit in this century will bring an explosion of power, faith and glory, which will cover the earth with miracles, signs, wonders, wealth, health, and more. We arc living the times of the fullness of God, where the former and latter glory will join and become more powerful and explosive. We are blessed to live in this generation and to be part of this outpouring of the Holy Spirit.

> *We must be willing to make room for the Holy Spirit to move explosively in our lives and ministries.*

PURPOSES OF THE OUTPOURING OF THE HOLY SPIRIT

Like everything God does, the outpouring of His Spirit has a definite, specific and clear purpose. Everything in Him is related to His plan of salvation for man, to reconcile us with our Creator and to give us dominion over the earth. God wants to us to return to His original plan. For the same reason, the purposes of His outpouring are:

- ### Impact a Community, city and/or country

    One of the purposes of baptism with the Holy Spirit is to empower the believer to serve God, but the outpouring includes more than that. It deals with causing a spiritual impact on communities, cities and nations. That impact is of such magnitude that it causes a change in the history of that region; transforming hearts, taking drug addicts and alcoholics out of their vices, and giving meaning and purpose to people. Where there is an outpouring of the Spirit, bars close, prisons are emptied and economic prosperity is released in the region.

■ Remove demonic powers

In every place where an outpouring of the Spirit occurs, the demonic powers that dominate over that region are removed. The principalities of death, suicide, hatred, racism, violence, sexual immorality, family disintegration, depression and human degeneration are brought down. Witchcraft, sorcery, spiritism, atheism, materialism and many more are cast out. As a result, the Kingdom of God expands with miracles, signs and wonders.

This brings a great change in people's behavior. Where once there were hard hearts that rejected the love of God, there are now desperate people running to Him. Changes in people are evident, spiritual bonds are broken and what Jesus said is fulfilled: *"The Spirit of the Lord is upon Me, because He has anointed Me to preach the gospel to the poor; He has sent Me to heal the brokenhearted, to proclaim liberty to the captives and recovery of sight to the blind, to set at liberty those who are oppressed"* (Luke 4:18).

- **Impact the world with the good news of the Kingdom**

    An essential part of the outpouring of the Holy Spirit's purpose is the preaching of the gospel. That's why Jesus spoke to His disciples about the terrible signs that will come before the end. He promised them that in the midst of the multiplication of evil, *"This gospel of the kingdom will be preached in all the world as a witness to all the nations, and then the end will come"* (Matthew 24:14).

    When an outpouring of the Spirit occurs, a global transformation takes place; there are miracles, prosperity and a change in all aspects of life. The outpouring of the Holy Spirit comes to impact the world with the message of the gospel of the Kingdom. People receive salvation and pass from the kingdom of darkness to the Kingdom of light; so that they may live heaven on earth. This is proven because there are fewer places now where the gospel of the Kingdom has not been preached.

MOBILIZATION OF THE ARMY OF GOD ON THE EARTH

Now that we understand the purpose of the outpouring of the Holy Spirit, let's see how the mobilization of God's army is performed and what we should do. Here are some key steps:

- **Commission and mobilize God's people**

True outpouring is an explosion that sets the Church in motion. Every believer must be mobilized and commissioned to perform miracles, signs and wonders, and to be witnesses of Christ Jesus in the streets, schools, universities, offices, banks, and everywhere they go.

What does it mean to mobilize? it is to put something or someone into movement. In this case, it is a question of mobilizing the army of God, made up of those who are truly born again, to fill them with the Holy Spirit and power, and prepare them for battle.

> *If we do not commission and mobilize people, then the purpose of the outpouring is lost.*

If the outpouring of the Holy Spirit only serves for you to spend a nice time in church, then there is no valid reason for it to happen. Thus, if service ends, everything remains the same and nobody is transformed, then that outpouring was in vain. Apart from discerning its season, our mission should be to carry the same outpouring and overflow out of the four walls of the church, preaching the gospel and demonstrating the supernatural power of God to the world.

There are several reasons why the Church should be mobilized. These are the most important:

- *The second coming of the Lord is near.* All the signs have been fulfilled and we know we are living in the cycle of the end times.

- *There is a great sense of urgency.* When the people of God are empowered, but the message is not preached with a sense of urgency, they do not mobilize. That is why the prophetic voice of today imparts that drive to us, because the times are coming to an end.

- *The reality of hell.* If we do not believe that hell is real we will not have urgency to evangelize. Jesus spoke more of hell than of heaven, because even heaven is temporary, but hell is eternal.

In what areas should we be mobilized? The mobilization that leads us to be ready for battle includes such important areas as: prayer, fasting, evangelism, manifestation of miracles, signs, wonders, deliverance, finances for the Kingdom, and so on.

■ Gather the greatest harvest of souls ever seen

"Jesus said to them: My food is to do the will of Him who sent Me, and to finish His work. Do you not say, 'There are still four months and then comes the harvest'? Behold, I say to you, lift up your eyes and look at the fields, for they

are already white for harvest" (John 4:34-35). The outpouring of the Spirit prepares people's hearts to receive the message of salvation. God's army on earth—all of us who have recognized Jesus as our Lord and Savior, and who have been baptized with the Holy Spirit—must be ready to mobilize and gather that great harvest.

- **Consolidate the body of Christ**

Once people have accepted Christ in their hearts, we must affirm them in the faith (Acts 16: 5). How? Encouraging them to receive the baptism in waters and with the Holy Spirit, teaching the foundation of life in God and working to help them achieve spiritual maturity. In addition, we must activate their gifts, anointing, faith and leadership abilities. To consolidate a believer in faith is to lead him to operate in the supernatural; otherwise their faith will be founded on theories, just like any other religion. To consolidate the people is also to assign them to operate in their calling, purpose, assignment and in their territory. It means putting them to work in unity, as part of the body of Christ. *"For in it the righteousness of God is revealed from faith to faith; as it is written: The just shall live by faith"* (Romans 1:17).

- **Equip and empower people**

For the Lord's army to mobilize, we must teach, train and equip ministries, pastors and leaders. We must activate them and impart them so that they can go to schools, offices, sports centers, museums, universities, prisons and more as witnesses of Jesus Christ. We must teach them to establish the righteousness of Jesus in their cities. It should be clear that no service, training course, retreat, etc., should end without a call to the lost and an opportunity to demonstrate the power of God. If we know the purpose of His outpouring and that our duty is to activate and mobilize believers to carry the Spirit's "bubbling" to the world, then these must be the main parts of every service.

This is something I do wherever I go. Unfortunately, many leaders are afraid of activating their leaders and believers because when a person is empowered, he leans toward independence. However, I do not think that's the point. It is true that some leave, and that is unfortunate, but it is much worse if we stop the outpouring of the Spirit or become the only ones who can operate the power of God, when it was promised to all.

Most Christian conferences and retreats being held today were made to teach the Word, but not to empower or mobilize the people. They bless the people, but they do not activate them. Even pastors' associations come together to socialize, but they do not develop mobilization strategies for God's army in their regions or countries. However, the Lord demands that every believer be empowered, mobilized, commissioned, and sent to demonstrate His Kingdom and power. We cannot afford to have a person in our congregation doing nothing, because we will be judged for them. Each conference should serve to empower, activate and mobilize the body of Christ to evangelize, working miracles, healing the sick and cast out demons.

We have proof of this in our ministry. Recently, a woman living in Philadelphia told us what happened in her life after attending our annual conference in Miami:

"My name is Janet and I live in Philadelphia, Pennsylvania (USA). Fourteen years ago, my twin pregnancy had complications. I suffered a heart attack so serious it left me disabled me, and I was put on a waiting list for a heart transplant. I suffered from sudden fainting spells, could not walk long distances, and had sleep sitting up to keep my lungs from filling with liquid. Because of that I took many medications. At first I resigned myself and got used to living like this; but after a few years I began to grow desperate for God to touch me and heal me.

"So, I came to the Conference of the Apostolic and Prophetic (CAP) for the first time. In one of the sessions, Apostle Maldonado was preaching, when he suddenly said: 'The Holy Spirit is interrupting, because He wants to heal His people'. The apostle started declaring a wave of creative miracles, and that the fire and the angels of God would touch the sick; and I felt that fire! The Holy Spirit poured His power over me and I felt His fire run through my body. I had never experienced anything like it! My body was consumed under the fire and glory of God. At that moment, I realized that I could no longer be tied to my way of thinking. That was beyond my reason! Immediately, I began to feel stronger and healthier.

"When I returned to Philadelphia I went to the doctor for a routine checkup. Then, my cardiologist told me he was withdrawing from the transplant waiting list, because my heart was in perfect condition. I was completely healed! The doctors could not understand what had happened. Science has no explanation for my healing. I can only say that it was the supernatural power of God."

However, the testimony does not end there, because it is not just that people experience the power of God, but that they are empowered to bring that power to other areas and other people. Janet brought that power to Philadelphia and this is what she continues to share:

"After my healing, I completely dedicated myself to starting a company. We started an image consultant with only fifteen thousand dollars, one employee and a doctor. We followed the teachings of apostle Maldonado to the letter, about seeking the guidance of the Holy Spirit, sowing in the Kingdom, resting in God and believing in spiritual acceleration. I did all this and God worked. Our business began to grow aggressively. Six months later, we had half a million dollars in profits. We remain faithful in our tithes and sowing in the Kingdom, and now our business is quoted in 2.7 million dollars; we have 23 employees and 3 surgeons.

"We stopped renting to have our own offices, with state-of-the-art equipment, located in the sixth richest county in the United States. We are the only Latino business in the area. There we carry the power of God. Recently, a lady came to our clinic for a consultation. We learned that her five-year-old daughter had cancer, so we prayed for her and she was healed by the power of God! We have also seen restored marriages. The Holy Spirit is in our clinic and operates His power through us!"

HOW TO RECEIVE AN OUTPOURING OF THE HOLY SPIRIT

Amid so many problems, difficulties and the great amount of misinformation we receive every day, we often fail to look for what really matters. The outpouring of the Holy Spirit should be a priority for us. From there, every problem, impossibility or crisis will come under the control of the Spirit and will be solved by the power of God. How do we receive that outpouring? Let's look at some contexts that reflect this outpouring:

- **Perplexities**

Many people come to have an encounter with the supernatural when they have no choice, and are suffering from a terminal illness, a family problem, or a seemingly-impossible situation that leaves them perplexed and not knowing what to do. It is then they realize that only God can change their reality.

> *Perplexity always captures man's attention to seek God.*

■ Desperation for more from God

"As the deer pants for the water brooks, so pants my soul for You, O God. My soul thirsts for God, for the living God. When shall I come and appear before God?" (Psalms 42:1-2). When we are tired the attacks of the devil and of situations that defeat us, when people are not changing or turning away from their rebellion against God, then we enter a desperation for a divine intervention, for an outpouring of His Spirit.

And you, are you happy with what God did in the past? Are you content just reading miracle stories in the Bible or do you want to be a part of those miracles? Are you satisfied with traditional Christianity or are you desperate for a change? Do you know deep inside that there is more to life than what you have experienced and that we are in the middle of a spiritual awakening? Do you want a revival in your life? Do you want an awakening in your family and in your city? Are you willing to pay the price to be used by God with miracles, signs and wonders? If you are desperate for a change or a revival, the Spirit is willing to pour Himself over you, your family, your ministry and your city.

> *The cross, the Holy Spirit, and the supernatural are what set Christianity apart from other religions.*

■ A complete surrender to the Holy Spirit

The anointing and the power of the Holy Spirit are two of the ways God works through a man, and both operate by the law of Exchange, *"For He whom God has sent speaks the words of God, for God does not give the Spirit by measure"* (John 3:34). God gives us anointing and power without measure, but it depends on us how much we receive by the priority we give to that impartation. The more we surrender to the Holy Spirit, the more we will have of Him. That is why Paul said: *"I have been crucified with Christ; it is no longer I who live, but Christ lives in me; and the life which I now live in the flesh I live by faith in the Son of God, who loved me and gave Himself for me"* (Galatians 2:20).

The measure of the Holy Spirit and power that you have are a mark of how much of yourself of you have surrendered to God. If you have only given fifty percent, that is the space available in your spirit, and the limit of anointing and power you can receive. Another way of saying it is that you harvest in proportion to what you sow; no more and no less. If you give yourself completely to the Holy Spirit, He will give Himself entirely to you.

We all have areas to surrender to God: our rights, natural fears, insecurities, jealousy and of course, the flesh. We must let go of these, of entertaining wicked thoughts, anger, unforgiveness, stubbornness, old scars, sexual immorality... We must let it all go to make room for more of Spirit.

You must make the decision to give more of yourself and ask for more from Him; to want more of Him and less of you. Jesus was so hungry for the Father's will that He died to Himself, to such a degree that the Father give Him both the anointing and the spirit of power without measure.

OUTPOURING AND REVIVAL

I want to close this chapter by leaving you with the conviction that we can all carry and release an outpouring. The Holy Spirit is one and the same for all. That means that every believer has the same potential as Peter, Paul or the best preacher of our century. We all have the same capacity to be used. No matter your gender, nationality, race or social status, you can be used by the Holy Spirit now.

I can give you testimony of thousands of people that I have activated and now move with the power of the Holy Spirit. They are used in miracles, signs, marvels, casting out demons or raising the dead, because we all have the same rights in God. When you go to your workplace, office or school, expect to see miracles, healings, signs, wonders, and supernatural provision.

> *As believers, we are called to continue the legacy of Jesus.*

When Jesus said, "Most assuredly, I say to you, he who believes in Me, the works that I do he will do also; and greater works than these he will do, because I go to My Father" (John 14:12), is talking about the mark that should distinguish a believer and every Christian.

Throughout history there have been different models of revival and each has presented a different emphasis. For example, in Pensacola, Florida (USA) a revival occurred which emphasized the presence and glory of God; people could not resist His presence! It was something so strong and tangible that men and women fell on their knees, worshiping and acknowledging the Lord. This even happened in the streets. There we saw the prophetic emphasis and God spoke precisely through His servants the prophets.

We have also experienced outpourings where the emphasis has been on power. In them we saw God working miracles, signs and wonders in a massive way. However, when the outpouring is focused on bringing times of refreshment, then joy and laughter come upon the people of God. This is one of the most criticized and least-understood types of outpouring. Another outpour is on the salvation of souls, which reveals the heart of God, for the ultimate purpose is to reconcile His children for the Kingdom. A different emphasis points to finances and the transfer of riches from the wicked to the righteous. Today we often see this outpouring of the Holy Spirit, because wherever He moves the riches go. Two other types of are transformation of the heart, and deliverance, which are also important.

The point is, throughout the centuries of the Church, we have seen different ways the Spirit of God manifests, but in the end times, the outpouring includes everything: miracles, signs, wonders, prophecies, power, salvation of souls, transfer of finances, transformation of the heart, and deliverance. This is the kind of movement I carry, so in our ministry we have testimonies of movements that include them all.

> *The outpouring of this final time will bear witness to the second coming of Christ and prepare the bride for His glory.*

By the grace of God I am one of the custodians of the supernatural movement in the world. A custodian is one who has the keys to access something specific, in this case, for the spiritual realm. I give Him all the glory for trusting me with something that builds up the body of Christ in a special way. The following is a testimony that confirms what I have just explained.

"My name is Sam, and I am from South Africa. A while ago, apostle Maldonado and his team came to East London, to minister at a conference called 'Days of Glory'. I could not attend, but I watched the TV broadcast. One night, while the apostle directed worship, suddenly the glory of God descended upon all, and he could not continue to minister. It seemed the entire assembly had a supernatural encounter with God. Then the apostle said: 'Those who watch on television, begin to pray in tongues because you too will have encounters with the Lord'. I obeyed and suddenly I felt that Jesus himself had entered my room. I fell before Him and could not look at His face because His glory was so powerful. Then He began to tell me everything He wanted me to do. My life changed since that encounter. Suddenly my spirit strengthened and I was activated and empowered by the Holy Spirit. So I took that impartation, started moving in the power of God and began a revival in my city.

"I started a ministry in the city of Mthatha, in the province of Eastern Cape, South Africa, an area known for witchcraft and powers that have taken that region. Many oppressed people live there and schools teach witchcraft as a school subject. They live a lie, trying to mix Christianity and the rituals of witchcraft. In the morning, the pastors preach with the Bible in their hands, but in the afternoon, they lead witchcraft ceremonies, sacrificing cows and goats to their dead ancestors. They even try to explain it by saying that services in the church are a religious belief and that witchcraft is a cultural belief.

"I feel the burden and compassion of the Holy Spirit to deliver the captives in my city. My ministry is focused on serving the community, prisoners, families and the homeless. One day I went to the general hospital of the city and the Holy Spirit led me to the area of psychiatry. I asked permission from the hospital staff to come in, and when I told them what I was doing, everyone laughed at me. They brought me to their worst patient, the most violent of them all.

"When I saw him, I told him that Jesus Christ would set him free. There were so many evil spirits in him! I remember praying for his deliverance, when he jumped out of his seat and threw himself at me trying to beat me and strangle me, but he could not even touch me. The Holy Spirit protected me! After he accepted Christ as His Savior, I led him to renounce every evil spirit and be set free. He manifested and vomited with every spirit I mentioned. When he had finished, his entire look changed completely. All the aggression and violence were gone and for the first time in years, the man could hold a coherent conversation without being tied up or medicated.

"He has now been discharged and is coming to church! The hospital staff cannot believe it. They say that this deliverance was possible only by the power of God. I am currently doing a weekly radio program, where I pray for my city and my country, and I am saturating the air with the Word of God; but this is just the beginning. I am empowered and activated to bring a revival and outpouring of the Holy Spirit to my city, Eastern Cape."

The outpouring of the Holy Spirit this season will be something never seen before. It will overcome human reason and control, because it is the one that anticipates the second coming of the Lord, and is the preparation for the manifestation of His glory.

The testimony of the Apostle Jorge Ledesma, from the city of Resistencia, province of Chaco, in Argentina, South America, perfectly illustrates the need to walk under the anointing of the Holy Spirit. Despite having witnessed some of the most important revivals in the United States and South America, he noticed there was a great spiritual emptiness in his church that would not let him progress. Guided by the Spirit of God and connected with our ministry, this is what happened:

"Since the first time I had contact with the King Jesus Ministry, I realized that our church had abandoned the Holy Spirit. I also discovered the power of an apostolic church, but most of all I witnessed paternity! This is what transformed my life, that of my family and our ministry.

"When we came under the spiritual cover of Apostle Maldonado, our services changed and the church shifted. We jumped into the river of the Spirit! In just five years, growth figures multiplied. Today we gather more than 25 thousand people every Sunday and we continue to grow. We have built a new sanctuary with capacity for 18 thousand people, debt-free. In addition, we offer spiritual coverage to other pastors and they also grow mightily.

"Since the first-time Apostle Maldonado visited us, the church's finances doubled in a matter of days, with the same number of people! It is important to emphasize that we are located in one of the poorest provinces of Argentina, which turns financial miracles and our great building into a monument to the power of God.

"The old religious structures were overthrown by the river of fresh revelation we received in each Supernatural School of the Fivefold Ministry, and in each Conference of the Apostolic and Prophetic (CAP). Since we began to walk in the supernatural power of God, we have witnessed creative miracles. For example, people with no ear or ear canal can now hear clearly; women who had their uterus removed now become pregnant; destroyed vertebrae are restored in minutes, etc. In addition, financial miracles multiplied. Money appears in the bank accounts of our members, and people's debts are miraculously canceled."

As we can see, the presence of the Holy Spirit is able to transform the environment where we live. What happens in Argentina is happening in other cities and nations, which are being transformed by the supernatural power of the Spirit of God. We must be expecting His outpouring.

As if that were not enough, the same thing is happening in Europe, at the seat of Catholicism. God is removing the old structures and bringing His kingdom and His supernatural power to this generation. I invite you to know this other powerful testimony:

"I am Apostle Enzo Incontro, pastor of the Missione Paradiso church, of Catania, Sicily, Italy. My first encounter with King Jesus Ministry happened in June of 2013, when I attended a Supernatural Fivefold Ministry School (SFMS). By that time, I was a young pastor and had recently taken over a historic church, almost 40 years old, with only 80 members. We were starting a mission in Catania, the largest city in the region, with 15 or 20 people in a rented theater.

"I was willing to leave my secular job, where I was an environmental manager, although I worked for Italian television and was at the top of my career. However, I did not mind leaving everything to serve the Lord full time. Unfortunately, I was frustrated to see that the congregation was not growing.

"So, my wife and I decided to travel to Miami. Although we were full of doubts and skepticism, God had a great surprise for us. From the first preaching we were shocked to hear of supernatural transformation. It was as if scales fell from my eyes. This pair of Italian skeptics, were exposed to such a weight of glory that we fell to the ground under His power. Although we totally rejected any manifestation of the Holy Spirit, we ended up lying on the floor, with no strength to do anything other than cry and thank God.

"That same day, Apostle Maldonado approached us during lunch and said to me, 'Son, you need a father.' Through the Holy Spirit, He told me things I would never have imagined I would receive from a man I had just met. Since then, my ministry has changed radically. The Holy Spirit began to move freely, after receiving the impartation of who later became my spiritual father.

"With simplicity of heart, I must say that in just four years, a small group of 15 members now brings together almost a thousand people. The Holy Spirit has led us to establish daughter churches and new missions in the rest of Italy. We recently bought, a plot of almost ten thousand square meters in the center of Catania, completely debt-free! Its value is 200 thousand euros, when its original value was 800 thousand euros. On this terrain, we are building a new temple with a capacity for

1,500 people. Also, we continue to impact the country through our TV program that is broadcast on Italian television."

> *The movement of the end times will be the very glory of God, with all things included.*

We must be expecting an outpouring of the Spirit in our home, family and church, today. Only then will we see the glory of God filling the earth.

We are so blessed to live in this time, where we can see the greatest movement of the Lord and His sovereign intervention in the Church. Let us not be like Jerusalem who failed to recognize the time of the visitation of God. Instead, let us watch and give complete freedom and room to the Holy Spirit in our midst.

4

The Revelation of Gift of Tongues

In modern Christian circles, it is becoming less common to hear about praying, worshiping or speaking in spiritual tongues. They are simply denied or rejected. Tongues are no longer seen as a necessity, nor are they sought as the gift of the Spirit that every believer should long for. However, in reviewing Scripture, we see the believers of the early Church were continually filled with the Holy Spirit and spoke in other tongues. The exercise of this gift was a pattern among early Christians because it was a sign of Jesus' promise to us, of being empowered to fulfill the great commission.

The rejection of the things of the Spirit has caused the Church of Jesus to lose its drive. There is little spiritual activity, and this includes exercising the gift of tongues. Apostle Paul spoke to the Corinthians about this and said: *"Now concerning spiritual gifts, brethren, I do not want you to be ignorant"* (1 Corinthians 12:1). The word "spiritual" alludes to something supernatural. God is Spirit; indeed, the Bible says that He is the Father of spirits (Hebrews 12:9). So, we can not ignore the things of the Spirit because it would be like ignoring God Himself. Moreover, the original state of man is spiritual, not physical, because man comes from God.

> **The Lord wants us to know the realm of the spirit and walk in it, just as well or more than the natural one.**

The spiritual realm is divided into two: the realm of the Holy Spirit and the satanic realm. Every believer needs to know the realm of the Spirit. It is only when we return to the dimension of the spirit that we can know ourselves and God.

In his first letter to the Corinthians, Apostle Paul describes the different gifts, ministries and operations. He affirms that, "The manifestation of the Spirit is given to each one for the profit of all" (1 Corinthians 12:7). A manifestation refers to something visible, to an open demonstration of the gift. This means that the manifestation of the Spirit is given to every believer to minister to God, and to edify our brothers and sisters in Christ.

The gifts of the Holy Spirit come in different manifestations, and we can classify them into three groups:

- *Gifts of revelation:* Here we find words of wisdom and science, as well as the discernment of Spirits.

- *Gifts of power:* Referring to the different manifestations of faith, healings and miracles.

- *Gifts of inspiration:* They include prophecies, various genres of tongues, as well as the interpretation of tongues.

All manifestations of the Holy Spirit are connected to a specific moment or situation in which they are needed. For example, no one needs the gift of healing if they are not sick, nor the gift of miracles if they do not have an impossible circumstance. If someone tries to operate a gift when it is not needed, it will grieve the Holy Spirit. He is not an object to play with, remember that He is a person and is God Himself. Each of the His gifts has a purpose and an area of operation, and if you do not understand the manifestation of a particular gift, it will not profit you.

In the area of inspirational gifts, let's focus on studying the gift of tongues. We will see what it is, how it operates, its different genres, the blessings that come from praying in spiritual tongues, and how to cooperate with the Holy Spirit to receive this gift.

THE ORIGIN OF THE TONGUES OF THE SPIRIT

The first reference of tongues in the Scriptures is found in the book of Genesis. The Bible says that, *"Now the whole earth had one language and one speech"* (Genesis 11:1). However, in the same chapter we read that men said: *"Come, let us build ourselves a city, and a tower whose top is in the heavens; let us make a name for ourselves"* (v. 4); God was not pleased with their plan, which is why He said: *"Come, let Us go down and there confuse their language, that they may not understand one another's speech"* (v. 7). A second reference is seen here, then He descended and released the speaking of tongues upon them, to prevent the people from building the monument of their pride; the tower of Babel.

From that moment on, language became a barrier between peoples. The term "Babel" means confusion and disorder, and is attributed to a place where many speak without understanding, as the fruit of evil and pride. As a result, a communication problem began on the earth, where everyone spoke so differently that it was impossible to understand each other. It is believed that this is the origin of the tongues, which gave birth to languages as we know them today. Therefore, we need to learn different languages and translate the message of the cross, to take the gospel to all the nations of the earth, and it can be understood.

The third reference to "tongues" or speech appears in the book of Hebrews. *"When the Day of Pentecost had fully come, they were all with one accord in one place. And suddenly there came a sound from heaven, as of a rushing mighty wind, and it filled the whole house where they were sitting. Then there appeared to them divided tongues, as of fire, and one sat upon each of them. And they were all filled with the Holy Spirit and began to speak with other tongues, as the Spirit gave them utterance"* (Acts 2:1-4). Thanks to this supernatural event of the Holy Spirit, all nations present in Jerusalem heard and understood the gospel in their own language.

Who received the gift of tongues were Hebrews, but suddenly, each of the peoples gathered there heard them speak in their own language. *"'And how is it that we hear, each in our own language in which we were born? Parthians and Medes and Elamites, those dwelling in Mesopotamia, Judea and Cappadocia, Pontus and Asia, Phrygia and Pamphylia, Egypt and the parts of Libya adjoining Cyrene, visitors from Rome, both Jews and proselytes, Cretans and Arabs—we hear them speaking in our own tongues the wonderful works of God.' So they were all amazed and perplexed, saying to one another: Whatever could this mean?"* (Acts 2:8-12). This is the equivalent of someone who speaks only German coming to visit our church, and while I speak in English, he listens to me in perfect German, though I do not even know that language. That's what happened to them.

> *To speak in other tongues was a release of the supernatural that reversed what had happened in the tower of Babel.*

At Pentecost, Jews and Gentiles accepted Jesus and became one. What happened demonstrates the power of God and the scope of the gospel of the Kingdom through the gift of tongues. Suddenly, without having known or studied any of these languages, the disciples of Christ knew the language of all these people and spoke to them as easily as natives.

> *To speak in tongues was a sign for the unbelieving.*

But the Bible also refers to another type of tongues. This is a gift given also by the Holy Spirit, but which does not involve any known human language. Rather, it deals with a divine, spiritual, supernatural language. It is the gift of speaking various kinds of tongues (1 Corinthians 12:10) which appears as a manifestation of the Spirit.

The gift of divers kinds of tongues

The gift of various kinds of tongues is the ability to speak a language that the person who receives it has never studied, learned or known, nor could memorize. Clearly, the mind can not remember what it has not learned, which is why we understand that that gift is not natural. The term "various kinds of tongues" refers to a language never spoken on earth. It also suggests that there are different classes and levels of tongues. This means that, upon receiving that gift, the language spoken is not natural or human, but is supernatural and divine.

To speak different kinds of tongues is a supernatural phenomenon, because they were not learned in a mental way. It is something that goes beyond reason, and the human mind cannot explain it; therefore, the first time we speak in tongues, we find they have no meaning. That is precisely one way of knowing that we are moving in the realm of the supernatural. Our mind is not comfortable with the fact that our mouth speaks something it does not understand nor can reason. That is why it is necessary, when we begin to speak in leagues, that we pass over reason and intellect.

This is where many get stuck and do not progress or develop the gift, because they want to figure out what they speak. Any area of the supernatural that you try to reason will fail. For example, when I began to speak in tongues I found them very strange, because I did not understand them, and I thought they were a waste of time. But when I consulted Scripture about the revelation of this gift, I learned that, *"He who speaks in a tongue does not speak to men but to God, for no one understands him; however, in the spirit he speaks mysteries [...] For if I pray in a tongue, my spirit prays..."* (1 Corinthians 14:2, 14). My carnal mind will never truly understand the gift of tongues, but my spirit does.

> **Apart from God, man can not know the supernatural, as it is above and beyond natural laws.**

The first time we spoke in tongues we ask ourselves, "What am I saying?" We feel strange because our reason is not in control. Hence, we must be aware so that we don't let the enemy steal from us this gift of God. At that moment, a spiritual battle is waged. The enemy leads us to think naturally and we believe that we are crazy, that it is not something normal, that it's useless since we cannot understand it. Just remember that it comes from the Holy Spirit, and although it is a language we do not know in the natural, our inner being communicates directly with God.

Every time we try to reason spiritual tongues, we lose the ability to speak the language of God. The human mind cannnot remember what it has not previously grasped through the human intellect; however, the Holy Spirit can tell you certain things because He is not subject to time or reasoning.

> *Man does not usually believe in that which does not involve reason.*

When we speak in other tongues we declare something that is above and beyond reason, the natural, the present or the past we know. It is like bringing the future to the present, it is a way to accelerate the natural with the force of the supernatural. Therefore, begin to declare things that have not yet happened here, but that you know are the will of God.

We see this in the young people in our church. Some have their own prayer groups, what we call Houses of Peace (HOPs). They are filled with the Holy Spirit and minister to the other youth of the city with His power, leading people to experience God, see miracles and be free from demonic attachments. A leader in one of them received a young man who arrived desperate for a touch of God that would transform his life.

From the age of twelve, Cory was a boy who felt strong, dirty, and perverse impulses of lust. He began to watch pornography and masturbate, and over the years, depravity took place and Cory began to be drawn into bestialism. By the time he reached adolescence, he even molested his seven-year-old cousin, and abused him for months.

He watched pornography up to nine times a day. One day in a class at their school, a report was shown on what happens to victims of sexual abuse. At that moment he felt guilt, shame and condemnation, until he ran out of the school and headed home. He went into his room and cried to God to take that away. Over the next few days his addiction increased, but then a friend invited him to a House of Peace.

In desperation, he decided to give God a chance and went so that He would set him free. During the ministration at the HOP, he fell on his knees, crying before the Lord for his deliverance. One of the guys leading the meeting approached and began to pray for him. Cory says that at that moment he felt fire and the presence of God, and then began to sweat and feel very hot. The boy who ministered to him began to pray in tongues and suddenly said: "I see addictions." Though he tried, Cory could not stop crying, and instantly began to be free. He says he felt something remove a heavy burden off him.

For the first time in years, he felt that his heart was clean, and the day after that first encounter with the Holy Spirit, all those desires were gone. Cory began to have a relationship with God that same day, praying in tongues, fasting and looking for His presence. He now lives a free life and can spend hours worshiping God, while the Lord uses him to free others. Cory testifies that he recently entered a fast food business and asked the local staff por permission to pray for the people. When they said yes, Cory took the microphone behind the cash registers and began preaching the gospel. While doing so, the Holy Spirit gave words of knowledge to those present, and as a result, many were saved and experienced the power of God.

THE DIFFERENT TYPES OF TONGUES

"Though I speak with the tongues of men and of angels…" (1 Corinthians 13:1). This portion of Scripture gives us at least two types of tongues. Then we will talk about a third type that the Bible also mentions.

■ Human Tongues

Human tongues, also called "known tongues," are the ones I mentioned earlier when we talk about the tongues that people understood at Pentecost. They are the different languages that are spoken on the earth. The ability to speak them, without having previously learned them, comes from the Spirit and is given to preach to people in their own language. To speak those tongues is a manifestation of God's supernatural intervention, so that people believe in Him. However, that is the lowest level of the gift of tongues.

This happened and continues to occur many times, over the centuries, from the feast of Pentecost, when the Holy Spirit came upon the disciples of Jesus assembled in the upper room. Just like back then, there are many testimonies today from people who received a message in tongues from God. One of them is a woman who had no idea of the language she uttered—she only spoke in tongues at the moment—but the person who was listening recognized her language and clearly understood the message that God was giving her. This is a sign that the message is genuine.

Soon, the evangelist's ministry will begin to see those kinds of signs again. As they go through life, evangelists will speak of other human tongues, tongues that they never learned, but which people will recognize as their own language on the lips of a stranger. Then you will know that the message comes from God. That kind of sign causes the unconverted to be impacted and open their ears to the message of the Kingdom.

The Spirit of God will bring more manifestations of human tongues in these final times, and give us the power to preach in the language of the person who is listening. Thus, the impact will be greater and lead to genuine change; all because of the sign of God. Some people are difficult to reach without a demonstration of His power; either because of the hardness of their heart or because they speak little known languages or dialects. But since God always seeks the salvation, edification and blessing of His children, He makes a way. If someone's heart will not be touched through a miracle, a vision or a dream, He will do so through the gift of tongues.

> *All the gifts of the Holy Spirit are signs.*

One of the characteristics of this sign is that there is progression in the exercise of the gift. It means that it is increasing, and it is noticed when the speaker begins to understand the unknown language he or she is speaking, and can even interpret what others speak.

■ Angelic Tongues

Angelic tongues are the ones spoken by the angels in heaven. These correspond to the angelic visitations and bring angelic activity on earth. When we speak in angelic tongues, we reach the spiritual realm and feel the presence of those angels. I have seen when angels of the Lord are in a service. They like rays of light, and release supernatural activity into the atmosphere in their wake. The Scripture tells us, *"Are they not all ministering spirits sent forth to minister for those who will inherit salvation?"* (Hebrews 1:14).

Many believers lack knowledge about angels. They are spiritual beings sent for the Church and to each one of us. It is important that we know how to call them and what their functions are in our environment. In principle, they move when we declare the word of God, and we can give them orders as long as they are aligned with Scripture. David ordered them: *"Bless the Lord, you His angels, who excel in strength, who do His word, heeding the voice of His word."* (Psalms 103:20).

They will not move while we complain and murmur, but if we speak according to the Word, they will be activated. For example, I have commanded them to seek finances for the Kingdom, bring unbelievers, remove obstacles, or destroy works of the devil. I have also commanded them to wage war against principalities and powers, among many other things, according to what the Spirit has given me at a certain time; and they have done so.

When we begin to speak in angelic tongues we can see how renewed thoughts come to our minds. They are like an interpretation of what we are saying. The angels decode that message to our minds, so that what we are saying in the Spirit is what God is saying on earth now. That is the manifestation of heaven on earth! We do not choose the tongues that we are going to speak; only the Holy Spirit chooses them. But we speak them, declare and establish them on earth.

> **Each spiritual gift is intended to build the believer.**

God does not speak when people are not ready to listen. Therefore, if a message comes in tongues, the atmosphere must calm down for God to say what He wants. It is when His Spirit rests in us, that we suddenly know that He is going to speak.

One day I was teaching at a conference in Venezuela. The Lord had sent me to that country to demonstrate His supernatural power and the Holy Spirit had given me specific instructions of what He would do in His people. One night, as I preached, the atmosphere changed and I knew that God was going to do something at that time. I began to pray in tongues and the Holy Spirit spoke to me of special creative miracles, and that is what I ministered. Later I met a young man named Damian, who received a miracle during the conference and shared the following:

"The doctors had diagnosed me with varicocele disease and told me that I could not father children. My wife and I went to the conference, desperate to see God move. When Apostle Maldonado said that we had to touch the place where we had the problem, I confess that I was embarrassed because I had to touch my testicles, but I armed myself with courage and did so. Then the Apostle began to declare healing and said that we would feel pain in the place where we wanted to be healed. Instantly I felt a strong pain in my testicles. I turned to my wife and said, 'Now we can have children.' Weeks later, as we attended our church, the Holy Spirit confirmed me through a vision that would receive that blessing.

"A month later my wife began to experience general discomfort and vomiting. Since I had forgotten God's promise, I told her to get a cholesterol test, but my wife's faith was greater, and she told me she thought she was pregnant. So we went to the pharmacy to buy a pregnancy test and it came out positive! Today, we have a beautiful baby born after that word released by Apostle Maldonado, under the guidance of the Holy Spirit."

- **Unknown tongues**

The third type of tongues quoted from the Bible is found in 1 Corinthians 14:2, 4: "For he who speaks in a tongue does not speak to men but to God, for no one understands him; however, in the spirit he speaks mysteries […] He who speaks in a tongue edifies himself, but he who prophesies edifies the church". Strange tongues are those that contain the mysteries of God. Here, He uses our gift to speak in other tongues to reveal His mysteries on earth, in the time or season designated by Him.

> *To understand God's mysteries, we need the guidance of the Holy Spirit, His revelation or "rhema", and to pray constantly.*

The mysteries of God cannot be discovered by ourselves; He is the One who reveals them to us in His sovereignty. That is why, every time we want to discover them we must ask for revelation.

At this time, God will begin to do unusual supernatural things; ones that will seem strange to the Church. There is a new field of creative miracles for which we have no point of reference, because it goes beyond the doctrine and the known until now. However, this is not new and has happened before. For example, in 2 Kings 6:1-7 we see when the ax fell into the water, and by the word of Elisha the iron floated. Another example appears in Numbers 22:28 and it was when the false prophet's donkey spoke. This was no previous for any of these cases, but they happened. In the same way, today we need to be exercised in these three points of reference: the guidance, the rhema word of the Spirit, and continuous prayer in other tongues.

> *In the Old Testament, the evidence that someone had the Holy Spirit was that he or she prophesied. In the New Testament, the evidence is the person speaks in tongues of the Spirit.*

Most people pray in tongues to build themselves up. However, they never enter the dimension of praying in angelic tongues or strange tongues to know the mysteries of God. This happens because of either ignorance or ignoring the Spirit's call. For that reason, the mysteries remain hidden and the people of God perish.

According to the book of Acts, the early Church received the revelation of the Holy Spirit, exercised His power and thus shook the foundations of the cities where they proclaimed the gospel. They learned to move in the power of God because they continually prayed in tongues and were continually filled. The Holy Spirit was upon them, guided them, and moved through them to work miracles, signs and wonders.

> *The early Church lived in a continuous state of prayer in the Spirit; and it was easy to bring forth the manifestation of the Spirit of God and His power.*

Strange tongues are unknown to men, angels and the devil. When Satan was cast out of heaven, he left without knowing the mysteries of God. It was a part of the God he never knew; otherwise he would not have tried to take Christ to the cross. This was confirmed by Apostle Paul in his first letter to the Corinthians, when he said: *"But we speak the wisdom of God in a mystery, the hidden wisdom which God ordained before the ages for our glory, which none of the rulers of this age knew; for had they known, they would not have crucified the Lord of glory"* (1 Corinthians 2:7-8).

When we speak strange tongues, we do not address men but God. In fact, even angels do not understand the mysteries of the Father, because that is not part of their assignment. Lucifer was created by God as an angel of light and although he had access to certain things, he could not understand unknown tongues or mysteries; otherwise he would have known about the Lamb that was slain from before the foundation of the world. Instead, we have the Holy Spirit, and for Him nothing is unknown. From the moment we receive Him, we are authorized by God to know His mysteries.

When we speak strange tongues, new thoughts come to us, arriving out of nowhere like a flash, and bringing understanding in an instant. It is like being in a pitch-dark room and suddenly turning on the light; we immediately see clearly. What would have taken us years to understand, the Holy Spirit reveals it to us in a moment. He wants to reveal His mysteries to us about our daily life, of the next contract for work, our marriage, our family, church, relationships and disagreements; to show us what to do in complex circumstances that our reasoning and education fail to solve, because there is a mystery that is not obvious or a root that remains hidden. When we begin to pray in other tongues, God begins to give us the solutions for everything.

How do you access this type of revelation? One of the things I do is start talking in other tongues. These are the "normal" tongues—just to give them a name—which I speak regularly; but each time in prayer I push a little more in the spiritual world to speak strange tongues. My goal is always to reach that level where I can access the mysteries of God, what is available now. I never want to speak tongues just to build my spirit. My advice is that you do the same. Do not dedicate yourself to praying the same tongues, but ask the Holy Spirit to give you a new vocabulary, to enter deeper, in the realm that leads to the revelation of the mysteries of God.

> *Praying in strange tongues gives us immediate access to the spiritual world and the mysteries of God.*

God hid the mysteries in the third person of the Trinity, the Holy Spirit. He lives within us and guides us to uncover the mysteries of God, to release His will and power on earth. The devil hates when the Church prays in the Spirit, because he knows that believers will then have access to the heart of God. Jesus told His disciples: *"To you it has been given to know the mysteries of the kingdom of God, but to the rest it is given in parables, that 'Seeing they may not see, and hearing they may not understand'"* (Luke 8:10).

Communion with the Holy Spirit and access to the mysteries of God is of vital importance in carrying out the ministry He has assigned to us. Often, we encounter situations that we do not know how to solve. This is when we need heavenly intelligence, classified information, the supernatural knowledge that He possesses. The precious and blessed Spirit of God has come to guide us and pray the perfect will of God. That is why it is written that, *"...the Spirit also helps in our weaknesses. For we do not know what we should pray for as we ought, but the Spirit Himself makes intercession for us with groanings which cannot be uttered"* (Romans 8:26).

When we pray in tongues we have access to the spiritual dimension and the complete knowledge there is. There is a dimension that reason does not understand, but when the Holy Spirit comes upon us, then we "know" instantly. Several times I have encountered matters of ministry, family or finances that I have not known how to handle or resolve. Every time that happens to me I start to pray in the Spirit and, suddenly, without logic, I know what to do with total certainty and conviction. The Spirit gives me a clear and precise thought, and I know what direction to give that subject and how to act.

Apostle Paul said: "I thank my God I speak with tongues more than you all" (1 Corinthians 14:18). I follow his example, so 80 percent of my prayer life is in tongues of the Spirit. I adore, praise, intercede and ask in tongues.

Very rarely do I speak in Spanish or English because I know the access I have to the spiritual world through this heavenly language, "For everyone who asks receives, and he who seeks finds, and to him who knocks it will be opened" (Matthew 7:8).

> *Unknown tongues belong to the realm of mysteries.*

Many times, when I am preaching I start speaking in tongues. In response, God opens a new flow. Then the atmosphere changes, everything acquires new life and He brings revelation of what to do at that exact moment. Here I must emphasize that, in general, prophetic people understand the mystical side of God, but do not know the now of God. That is why many continue to prophesy, when God wants to do something different. It is because they do not understand that God lives and works in the eternal present, not in time.

When we speak in tongues we begin to know, see, perceive and feel in the spiritual realm. If it is a specific topic we are consulting God about, He will give us the exact revelation. Since Satan does not know what we are praying, he can not intervene in the answer either. It is not necessary that whoever prays is an apostle, prophet, pastor, teacher or evangelist; anyone can have access to the mysteries of God. The only requirement is that the person be born again and that the Holy Spirit lives in him or her.

THE BLESSINGS OF PRAYING IN TONGUES

1. Builds those who speaks them

When God created man, his spirit and mind were one, but after the fall they were separated. Now, even though we are born again, the mind has not reached our spirit. At its origin, the atmosphere of Eden was the glory of God, and man had one hundred percent of his cerebral faculties; he had the mind of Chris. However, a large percentage of our mental capacity died when Adam sinned, which is why our mind needs to catch up with our spirit. When we are born again, the Holy Spirit comes to us and makes a by pass to reason. Then, when we pray in the spirit, we have access to the rest of the mind. Praying in other tongues helps us to improve intellectually, so that our mind comes to be in the same point of understanding and wisdom as our spirit.

The Word says in 1 Corinthians 14:4 that, *"He who speaks in a tongue edifies himself, but he who prophesies edifies the church"*. This is confirmed in Judas 1:20 when it exhorts us saying, *"Beloved, building yourselves up on your most holy faith, praying in the Holy Spirit".* We are edified because praying in tongues accelerates the renewal of the mind. When we do this our intellectual capacity grows and our mind begins to reach our spirit. This is how we understand situations that make no sense. Every time we pray in tongues, we overcome the mental block that the fall of man imposed on us.

2. Expands the spiritual man in every believer

Praying in tongues abundantly, daily, increases the capacity to communicate with God and receive more from Him. That is, the natural man is reduced and the spiritual one, which is Christ in us, grows. It is the same as any cup; one may have a lot of room, but if it is full of something else, its available capacity decreases or is canceled. Praying in tongues leads us to empty the glass so all its capacity can be filled by God. If we do not pray in tongues, we make no room for Him, and He cannot release the blessings for our lives or meet our needs.

There are many people whose capacity was never filled or whose needs were never met, from not praying in tongues or because they have not seen the benefits of doing so. As we pray more in tongues we increase our capacity to receive more of the Word, holiness, love for God, passion to do His will, anointing, faith, signs, healings and miracles.

3. Gives us access to knowledge and divine revelations

Paul received revelation from God when he as taken up to heaven, but much of the wisdom he received about divine mysteries was through speaking in other tongues. That is why he said: *"And lest I should be exalted above measure by the abundance of the revelations, a thorn in the flesh was given to me, a messenger of Satan to buffet me, lest I be exalted above measure"* (2 Corinthians 12:7). Here Paul speaks of the thord he carried in his flesh (a physical affliction), but also lets us see the immensity of the revelations that God is willing to give us when we make room in our spirit for Him to speak.

When the above happens, things you could not imagine begin to flood your thoughts, and you start to turn those ideas around. You know you would never have thought of that. This is a sign that you have accessed knowledge and revelations that you did not previously believe existed. However, at no time does the believer determine the revelation that God will give him. It is God Himself who does it because He is the one who reveals the mysteries according to His time and will.

Whenever we want to enter the spiritual realm, and have access to knowledge and revelation, we must begin by praying in tongues. I guarantee you will receive revelation. That happens to me often. Whenever I go to the Scriptures and there is something I do not understand, I start praying in tongues and suddenly, I begin to receive knowledge and revelation. The same thing can happen to you! If you want more of the mind of God and walk in spiritual activity, push in the Spirit until you feel the change of dimension. Then you will feel how you are in sync with the mind of God.

One question I am often asked is this: "Can anyone have access to the mind and mysteries of God?" My answer is always the same: yes. Every believer who has been filled with the Holy Spirit has access to the mind and mysteries of God, because the Spirit's assignment is to teach us all things. He can prepare us, warn us and rid us of the traps of the enemy, but also reveal to us what is to come. We all have access to the future! Access to know what comes to the earth, the mysteries contained in Scripture and things we never knew before. All, through prayer in the language of the Holy Spirit.

4. Leads us to pray beyond our understanding

The natural mind is far below the spiritual one, and as long as our prayer remains on the mental plane, it cannot access the now of God. Our mind is handled in the realm of time, not in eternity. This means that the more we pray in the spirit, the less we will have of the natural mind. We become less conscious of ourselves and more aware of God, which causes revelation to begin to flow.

5. Increases spiritual activity

This is the point of reference by which we can measure spiritual activity in a person, church or ministry. When there is no prayer in tones, there is no spiritual activity, but when there is much prayer in tongues, there is also abundant moves of the Spirit. We can measure when a church has become lazier because the atmosphere is stagnant.

6. Provokes, stirs up, changes and edifies atmospheres

Today, when we want to build an atmosphere for the presence of God to descend, we turn to music. This has taken the place that corresponds to our voice and that is not correct. We are completely wrong! Only our voice can build the perfect atmosphere for God. That is why, when we speak in tongues, the atmosphere changes, because we speak the same language and the sound becomes one in the spirit.

> *The sound of the spirit is in our voice, not in an instrument.*

God creates environments, but we create atmospheres. When we pray in tongues we stir the spiritual dimension. It accelerates the atmosphere to a moment of now and unleashes a rhema that brings the voice of God. It generates a demand and activates the gifts of the Spirit, because it takes us beyond what we know.

Preachers impart to people from an atmosphere. That atmosphere is the presence of God. I am going to stop here and speak to you once more of my own experience. It has happened to me that when I arrive at a service, a nation or a church where there is no atmosphere to minister the Word, I see the dryness in the spirit and I feel stuck. When I speak of the atmosphere, I mean the spiritual realm. If there is no spiritual activity there is no movement. Then, when the Word is given, it is as if it bounces off the hearts of the people and changes no one.

I learned that lesson years ago, so whenever I come to a place where there is no atmosphere for miracles—to teach the Word and demonstrate the power of God—I put the people, especially the leadership, to pray in the spirit. This is something very important. I also call people who have not been baptized with the Holy Spirit, with the evidence of speaking in other tongues, to receive them right there. The moment they begin to speak in tongues, they provoke a quickened atmosphere of the presence of God. It is in these moments that the Holy Spirit wants to rise within us. He is about to do something new!

> *To establish the unity of the Spirit, we must first pray in tongues; this is how we become one voice, in complete unity.*

7. Accelerates breakthrough

When we pray in the spirit, we do it with advanced knowledge. This causes the breakthroughs to come faster and miracles to happen. What had been held back for years is suddenly activated. The unanswered prayer suddenis released and we receive an answer from God.

8. Keeps us aware and enables us to respond to spiritual movements

The person who prays a lot in tongues is spiritually sharp, and able to recognize the times and seasons of God. He is aware of what is about to happen. Someone who is connected to the spirit rarely gets caught by surprise, because he constantly in prayer, and God speaks to him.

9. It is the fastest way of connecting people with our anointing

When we pray in the Spirit, we skip reason. Sometimes we have prejudices or disbelief, which prevents us from receiving the mantle of the one who is ministering. But when we person begin praying in tongues, we not only connect with the anointing of the preacher, but begin to receive, because we bypass our mind—where the prejudice is—and overcome the spirit of unbelief. Often the enemy sends such spirits to prevent us from receiving miracles. Thus, when we cease to reason the supernatural, we connect to the anointing of the one who is imparting and everything flows better.

10. Our mindset changes

When we speak the same tongues, again and again, it is a sign that we are stuck. Therefore, we must push forward, to the new and fresh of the Spirit in the now. When we do, we begin to form a new mentality because we are speaking in new tongues. The important thing is always to keep pushing for the new, so that we do not get stuck in the patterns of the past.

11. It is a way of immediately accesing the spiritual realm

Praying, singing or worshiping in tongues gives us access to the realm of the Spirit. We always do in our church, in all services. The worship leaders sing in the spirit and the people join in.

> *The more we pray in the spirit, the more we can perceive in the spiritual realm.*

One of the things that singing in the spirit does is bring the presence of God quickly. It changes the atmosphere.

Praying in tongues gives us access to visions and increases our ability to see in the spirit. As we pray in tongues, we began to see something. Our spiritual perception increases, becomes more frequent, and we perceive more and more.

12. Allows us to prophesy

When we pray in tongues, we begin to declare prophecies, the word of the Lord and His will. This is why we pray in the spirit, to declare what comes out of the mouth of God. The opposite would be to assume what God says according to our own judgment.

Prophetic people understand the flow of the mysteries of God, although few know the "now" of God, which is not simply the present, but the eternal present, where there is neither past nor future. It is important to know how to discern it, because the prophetic always points to the future, but the now is not there. God's plan for the present lies in the realm of revelation. Prophets often speak of the future, but they do not know what God is doing in the now. However, a prophet who knows how to use the gift of tongues will also prophesy in the now.

According to my experience, when I go to pray for a person, I begin first in the Spirit, because I am aware of these principles. For example, if I feel I should prophesy over someone, I first pray in tongues because that gives me access to the spiritual world, to divine knowledge, to the future. Then I begin to prophesy and bring the future to the present. Suddenly thoughts come to me from God, and I declare them over that person. Also, when I am going to minister healings or miracles and realize that there is some obstacle, I pray in tones to remove it; and then declare what I am hearing from God. If I hear cancer, I declare that the cancer dissolves and disintegrates, in the name of Jesus. I declare the will of God and the prophetic word begins to come out of my mouth while I speak in tongues.

13. Raises the church's spiritual awareness

When the church prays in tongues corporatively, it is more conscious and aware of what happens in the spiritual realm. Praying in tongues keeps us alert and gives us the ability to respond to spiritual matters at all times.

14. Gives us access to the mysteries of God

Every time we pray in tongues, we push beyond what we usually pray, and enter the mysteries of God. This is the time when He is opening and revealing His mysteries to the church. The devil does not want us to know these mysteries, but we must continue pression on. How much power can the mysteries of God contain? Why does the enemy oppose the revealed mysteries? Well, I'll give you an example:

Each year, our ministry organizes an apostolic and prophetic conference in the city of Miami, where thousands of people from all over the world gather. One day, as we prepared for the event, we were strongly opposed by the threat of Hurricane Matthew, which grew so much that the Governor of Florida declared a state of emergency, just the day the conference was to begin. Because of this, all activity was suspended in the city. Matthew was coming directly to Miami at nearly 186 miles (300 km) per hour and bringing heavy rains. The city was preparing for destruction. People were scared, and the government could not do anything to avoid it, science either, but God did.

As an apostle of the city, I called the church to pray in the spirit, and to intercede for the will of God. We prayed and ordered the hurricane to turn to the sea. And that's what happened. When the impact on Miami seemed imminent, the hurricane swerved at the last moment and nothing happened. We were protected by the hand of God. When everyone expected chaos, we had peace and the Spirit supported us. Eventually, we were able to resume the event and God glorified Himself by manifesting in a powerful way. There was a great spiritual movement, angelic presence, miracles and signs of the presence and power of God and His Holy Spirit. More than 16,000 people from over eighty nations were present; and people from more than 100 nations followed the entire transmission via the Internet.

HOW TO RECEIVE THE GIFTS OF THE HOLY SPIRIT

So far, I'm sure you have received what I have been teaching, but there may be some questions left. For example, "How do I receive the gift of speaking in tongues? What should I do or not do?" Let me give you some practical advice. If you want to receive some gift of the Spirit you must:

1. Cooperarate with the Holy Spirit

The Spirit of God does not force us to do anything, but expects us to submit to His authority, influence, control and guidance as a voluntary act of obedience and faith. Some people resist prophecies, miracles, signs and tongues because they do not submit to the Spirit of God. When the Holy Spirit comes upon us, we must cooperate with Him, because all His manifestations and gifts are connected to our submission.

2. Yield your will to Him

Many people think that they do not need the Holy Spirit. In doing so, they completely cut off all supernatural activity. Jesus sent us the Spirit to work with Him. The Holy Spirit operates through us when we give way to Him and submit to His guidance. As long as you want to be in command and in control of everything, you cannot see the complete work of the Holy Spirit in your life. Jesus gave us an example of how to work together with His Spirit. As a man, He did not do His own will, but did only what the Father said to Him through the Spirit.

There is a remnant in this generation that is praying endlessly in other tongues, in order to bring the knowledge of more mysteries of God. My recommendation is that you join in. Surrender your will so that the Holy Spirit can manifest the will of the Father through you. By the law of exchange, when you yield the natural, He gives you the supernatural. Crucify your flesh so He can fill you with His presence and His power. Only then will you have access to greater areas of revelation of the mysteries of God and His plans for the end times.

HOW TO RECEIVE THE GIFT OF TONGUES

Jesus showed His hands and feet to His disciples so they could be convinced it was He who had risen. He breathed on them and received the Holy Spirit immediately. At that moment, they crossed the line from the Old to the New Testament. Scripture says, *"That if you confess with your mouth the Lord Jesus and believe in your heart that God has raised Him from the dead, you will be saved"* (Romans 10:9). However, they believed that

He had been raised from the dead because they received the holy breath. This is when the disciples received the eternal life of resurrection.

But there was more. The Holy Spirit had been promised to them when Jesus said, *"Behold, I send the Promise of My Father upon you; but tarry in the city of Jerusalem until you are endued with power from on high"* (Luke 24:49). The book of Acts speaks of this too and says: *"But you shall receive power when the Holy Spirit has come upon you; And you shall be witnesses to Me in Jerusalem, and in all Judea and Samaria, and to the end of the earth"* (Acts 1:8). Then came the day of Pentecost, *"And suddenly there came a sound from heaven, as of a rushing mighty wind, and it filled the whole house where they were sitting"* (Acts 2:2). This represents the baptism with the Holy Spirit. All of them had been filled with the Spirit of God, but this is when they experienced an outpour and received new tongues.

They received the supernatural power manifested. Everyone knew what had happened. They received boldness to be witnesses of Jesus. From chapter 2 of the book of Acts the Bible speaks about the day of Pentecost, because that day they were filled and baptized with the Holy Spirit. The initial sign of that baptism was that they spoke in other tongues. However, the Father's promise was to receive the power of the Holy Spirit. This means that speaking in tongues was the evidence of the power of the Holy Spirit. This means that speaking in tongues was evidence that power had come upon them.

If you want to receive the baptism with the Holy Spirit now, let me guide you through a few simple steps, following the teaching of Jesus. *"On the last day, that great day of the feast, Jesus stood and cried out, saying, 'If anyone thirsts, let him come to Me and drink. He who believes in Me, as the Scripture has said, out of his heart will flow rivers of living water.' But this He spoke concerning the Spirit, whom those believing in Him would receive; for the Holy Spirit was not yet given, because Jesus was not yet glorified"* (John 7:37-39). From these verses, we learn that we need to:

- Be thirsty
- Go to Jesus
- Drink from Him. (Open your mouth and drink of the invisible Spirit taht is being poured out over you). Do it now!
- Release that flow through your mouth. How? By speaking.

"If you then, being evil, know how to give good gifts to your children, how much more will your heavenly Father give the Holy Spirit to those who ask Him!" (Luke 11:13). Remember that the Holy Spirit will not force you to do anything. He will give you the words, but

you must speak them. The reason we do not speak in tongues is that we do not know what is going to come out of our mouth.

Many are afraid what they speak is coming out of themselves or of the devil; but first, know that the devil hates it when we speak in other tongues, because he does not want us to pray above what he can understand. If you are a child of God, do not be afraid to receive other spirits or something that does not come from Him, because the Bible says in Luke 11:13 that if you ask something of your natural father, he will not give you a scorpion. So, it is with the heavenly Father. If you ask the Holy Spirit, He will give it to you.

ACTIVATION PRAYER

Pray with me:

"Lord Jesus, I believe that You are the Son of God, that You died on the cross for my sins and rose from the dead. I believe that You forgive me and receive me as a child of God. If there is any resentment in my heart or lack of forgiveness against someone, I place it at Your feet. I forgive all people who have hurt or failed me, just as You forgive me. If I have practiced the occult, I recognize that it is a sin and I repent of it. In Your name, I renounce all contact with Satan and all hidden

powers. Now, I ask You to come to me and baptize me with the Holy Spirit. I present to You my body and ask You to use it as a temple of Your spirit. I give You my mouth to be an instrument of justice and worship You in new tongues. By faith I receive Your Spirit. Thank You, Lord. Amen!"

Now breathe and start talking in new tongues aloud. Move your lips and start talking. If nothing comes out, begin worshiping God in your own language and you will see that as you worship, the Holy Spirit will begin to give you other tongues. Do not be afraid or embarrassed if it sounds strange. You keep praying in the Spirit! Now, let me pray for you:

"Heavenly Father, in the name of Jesus, I release the Holy Spirit upon every person who is reading this book and has never been filled or baptized with Your Spirit. Holy Spirit, come and fill them with power. Right now, as initial evidence, I declare that they begin to speak in new tongues of the Spirit. Every person reading these lines begins to speak in new tongues now. Father, now they have access to the things of the Spirit. They have access to Your power. Father, in the name of Jesus, I ask You to allow them to see in the spirit; that they can see and perceive in the spiritual realm. I pray for those who are stuck in their prayer life. I release a fresh wave of Your anointing on them. Father, I shake the spiritual dimension in them so that the Holy Spirit invades them right now."

If you yield to Him, the Holy Spirit will fill you and give you the words to pray. He does not speak, you speak when He gives you the language; but it is a matter of faith. He will give you the words as you begin to speak them, but you must have the desire to speak in tongues.

"Father, I declare and release the gift of tongues upon Your people. In the name of Jesus Almighty, and I give You all the glory and praise, power and honor. Amen!"

About the Author

Apostle Guillermo Maldonado is the senior pastor and founder of King Jesus International Ministry (Ministerio Internacional El Rey Jesus), in Miami, Florida, a multicultural church considered to be one of the fastest growing in the United States. King Jesus Ministry, whose foundation is built upon the Word of God, prayer, and worship, currently has a membership of nearly seventeen thousand. The ministry also offers spiritual covering to a growing network of over three hundred churches that extends throughout the United States and globally in Latin America, Europe, Africa, Asia, and New Zealand, representing over six hundred thousand people. The building of kingdom leaders and the visible manifestations of God's supernatural power distinguish the ministry as the number of its members constantly multiplies.

Doctor Maldonado has authored over fifty books and manuals, many of which have been translated into other languages. Among his previous books are *How to Walk in the Supernatural Power of God*, *The Glory of God*, *The Kingdom of Power*, *Supernatural Transformation*, *Supernatural Deliverance*, and *Daily Encounters with God*, all of which are available in both English and Spanish. In addition, he preaches the message of Jesus Christ and

His redemptive power on his national and international television program, The Supernatural Now (Lo Sobrenatural Ahora), which airs on TBN, Daystar, the Church Channel, and fifty other networks, thus with a potential outreach and impact to more than two billion people across the world.

Apostle Maldonado has a doctorate in Christian Counseling from Vision International University and a master's degree in Practical Theology from Oral Roberts University. He resides in Miami, Florida, with his wife and ministry partner, Ana, and their two sons, Bryan and Ronald.

Have you been blessed by this product?

ENRICH YOUR LEADERSHIP

Log on to kingjesus.tv to have access to videos of preachings, music, conferences, testimonies and much more.

kingjesus.tv

Access the Supernatural, anywhere.